THE BATTLE FOR LAOS

VIETNAM'S PROXY WAR 1955–1975

STEPHEN EMERSON

Pen & Sword
MILITARY

First published in Great Britain in 2019 by
PEN AND SWORD MILITARY
an imprint of
Pen and Sword Books Ltd
47 Church Street
Barnsley
South Yorkshire S70 2AS

Copyright © Stephen Emerson, 2019

ISBN 978 1 52675 704 3

The right of Stephen Emerson to be identified as the author of this work
has been asserted in accordance with the Copyright, Designs and Patents Act 1988.

A CIP record for this book is available from the British Library All rights reserved.
No part of this book may be reproduced or transmitted in any form or by any means, electronic or mechanical including photocopying, recording or by any information storage and retrieval system, without permission from the Publisher in writing.

Every reasonable effort has been made to trace copyright holders of material reproduced in this book, but if any have been inadvertently overlooked the publishers will be pleased to hear from them.

Typeset by Aura Technology and Software Services, India
Maps and drawings by George Anderson
Printed and bound in England by TJ International Ltd., Padstow, Cornwall

Pen & Sword Books Ltd incorporates the imprints of Pen & Sword
Archaeology, Atlas, Aviation, Battleground, Discovery, Family History, History, Maritime, Military, Naval, Politics, Railways, Select, Social History, Transport, True Crime, Claymore Press, Frontline Books, Leo Cooper, Praetorian Press, Remember When, Seaforth Publishing and Wharncliffe.

For a complete list of Pen and Sword titles please contact
Pen and Sword Books Limited
47 Church Street, Barnsley, South Yorkshire, S70 2AS, England
email: enquiries@pen-and-sword.co.uk
website: www.pen-and-sword.co.uk

or

Pen and Sword Books
1950 Lawrence Rd, Havertown, PA 19083, USA
email: uspen-and-sword@casematepublishers

CONTENTS

Glossary	4
1. The Land of A Million Elephants	7
2. A Nation Divided	18
3. Into the Vietnamese Quagmire	36
4. Raising the Stakes	48
5. Escalation	70
6. The Beginning of the End	90
7. The Final Act	109
Notes	118
Bibliography	123
Index	125
Acknowledgements	128

LIST OF MAPS

Map 1:	Southeast Asia Theater	6
Map 2:	Laotian Theater	21
Map 3:	Northern Laos and the Plain of Jars	40
Map 4:	Northern Battlefield	58
Map 5:	Southern Panhandle	64
Map 6:	Operation About Face	83
Map 7:	Defending the Hmong Heartland	99
Map 8:	Southern Laos Area of Operations, 1971	104

GLOSSARY

Air America	CIA proprietary airline operating in Laos and Thailand
Arc Light	B-52 carpet bombing missions
ARVN	Army of the Republic of Vietnam (South Vietnam)
CAT	Civil Air Transport; forerunner to Air America
DMZ	demilitarized zone dividing North and South Vietnam
FAC	forward air controller; airborne observer targeting air strikes
FAR	Forces Armées du Royaome (Royal Armed Forces)
Group 559	North Vietnamese unit responsible for maintaining logistics network through southern Laos
ICC	International Control Commission, established under the Geneva Accords in 1954
Lima Site	U.S. designation for crude Laotian airstrips, each with its own distinctive number, e.g. Lima Site 32 (LS 32)
Long Chieng	Vang Pao's main base and CIA's paramilitary headquarters; often spelled "Long Tieng" in American reporting
MACV	Military Assistance Command Vietnam
Neutralists	military faction loyal to Kong Le; fought on both sides during the war
NVA	North Vietnamese Army
Operation Barrel Roll	Northern Laos operating area for U.S. interdiction and close air support to government forces
Operation Commando Hunt	U.S. interdiction effort in southern Laos replacing Steel Tiger operations; November 1968–March 1972
Operation Steel Tiger	Southern Laos operating area; U.S. interdiction effort against Ho Chi Minh Trail, April 1965–November 1968
Operation Tiger Hound	Southern Laos air operating area along the South Vietnamese northwest border that fell under MACV control
Operation Igloo White	Airborne sowing of more than 20,000 seismic and acoustic sensors along the Ho Chi Minh Trail to detect enemy movements
PARU	Police Armed Reaction Unit (Thailand); deployed as trainers in Laos
PDJ	French acronym for Plaines des Jarres (Plain of Jars)
Ravens	American contract forward air controllers; known by their call sign, Raven

Glossary

Grenade training for Hmong fighters in northern Laos in the early 1960s. (Photo Hmong Archives)

RLA	Royal Lao Army
RLAF	Royal Lao Air Force
SA-2	Soviet-made Guideline surface-to-air missile
SAM	surface-to-air missile
SLAM	Seek, Locate, Annihilate, and Monitor bombing missions along Lao–South Vietnamese border
SOS	special operations squadron (U.S. Air Force)
SOW	special operations wing (U.S. Air Force)
STOL	short takeoff and landing capability; reference to type of aircraft
Skyline Ridge	main defensive position just to the north of Long Chieng
TFS	tactical fighter squadron (U.S. Air Force)
White Star	name for U.S. Special Forces personnel (Green Berets)
Yankee Team	U.S. reconnaissance flights over Laos

The Battle For Laos: Vietnam's Proxy War 1955–1975

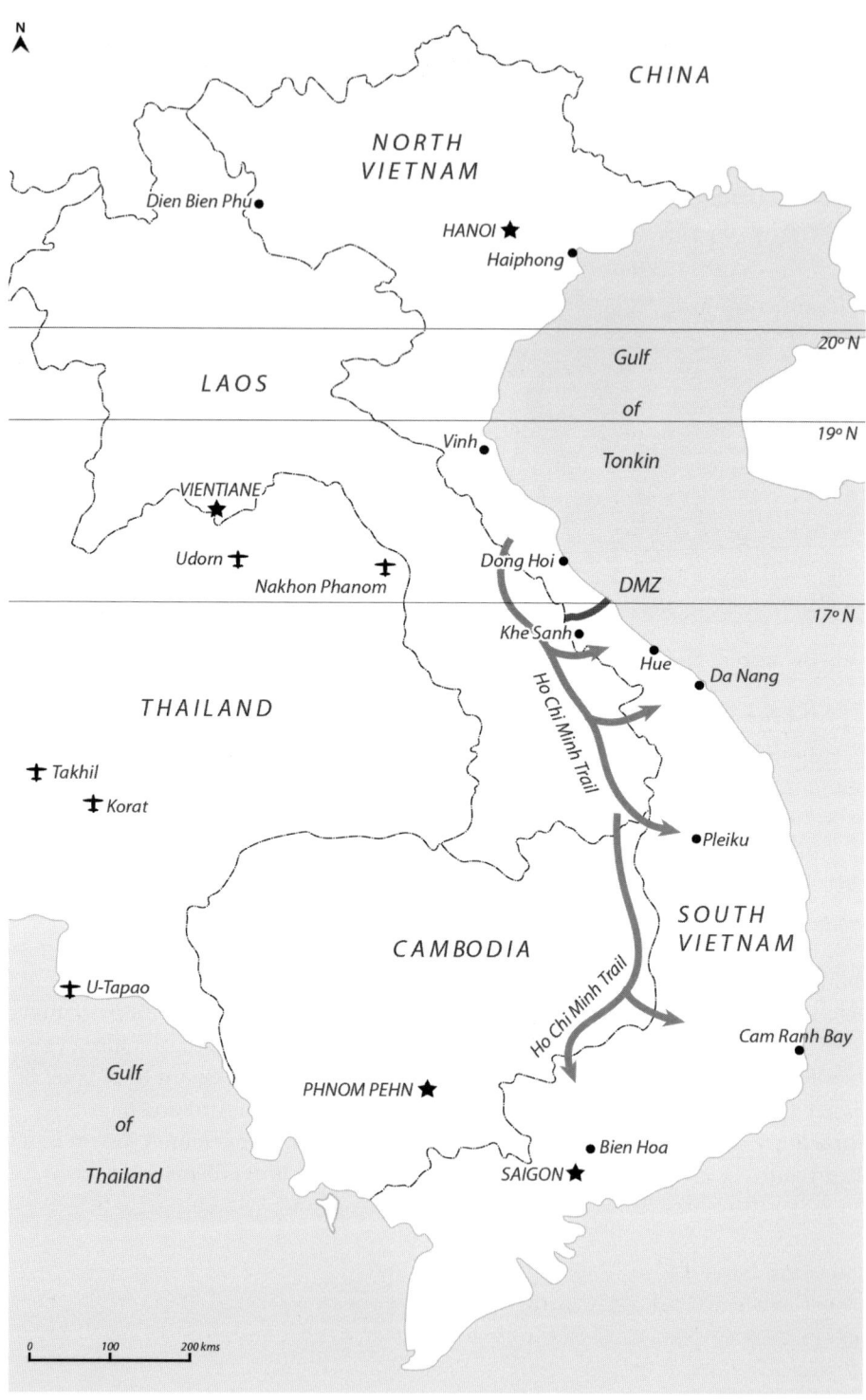

Southeast Asia Theater.

1. THE LAND OF A MILLION ELEPHANTS

Long the backwater of Southeast Asia, the remote and sparsely populated Kingdom of Laos—the land of a million elephants—would find itself by the early 1950s embroiled in the monumental struggle between East and West in Southeast Asia. While events in the northeast of the Indochinese peninsula would garner much more attention, the emerging war in Laos assumed increasing strategic importance for the United States in its effort to halt the spread of communism in the region. It, however, would be a very different kind of war. Largely unseen in this so-called "secret war," the Western-supported Royal Lao government forces would be pitted against the communist Pathet Lao and their North Vietnamese allies for the next 20 years as the landscape of Laos was transformed into yet another Cold War battleground. At the same time the escalating conflict in Vietnam and Hanoi's growing reliance on the Laotian panhandle for moving men and matériel into the south would further entangle Laos in the wider war in Southeast Asia. Thus, the future of Laotian people would become tied to competing regional and global foreign interests outside their control—a power struggle, whose outcome would ultimately seal their fate.

The Collapse of French Indochina
Following the end of World War II in the Pacific and the defeat of imperial Japan, indigenous nationalist movements rose up across Indochina to assert their right of self-determination. In early September 1945 Ho Chi Minh and his Indochinese Communist Party announced the creation of the Democratic Republic of Vietnam in Hanoi. Likewise, on October 12, 1945 Prince Phetsarath Ratanavongsa and his Lao Issara or Free Laos movement declared their independence from France and broke away from the French Union. None of this went over well with the French, who with the help of Allied forces systematically began reoccupying Indochina: Cochin China at the end of 1945, Tonkin by March 1946, and re-entering Vientiane in April. While the granting of internal autonomy to King Sisavang Vong of Luang Prabang seemed to assuage Lao nationalist sentiment, the outbreak of fighting between the Viet Minh and French in Hanoi in December 1946 signaled the start of the First Indochina War. Over the course of the next eight years the conflict would engulf the associated states of the French Union, pit France and its Western allies against the Viet Minh and its global communist allies, and turn Southeast Asia into a critical new Cold War battleground. It would also increasingly force Laotians to choose sides.

While the fighting became widespread as the Indochina conflict evolved—reaching into northern Laos, parts of central Annam, around Saigon, and even into the far south of the Mekong Delta—the most intense and decisive fighting of the war would be in the north's Tonkin region. It was here that for nearly eight years Ho Chi Minh's Viet Minh forces slugged it out against the French army and their French Union allies. From September 1945 to July 1954, Paris would send almost half a million men to the Indochina

French Indochina Chronology

1862–63	Cochin China (Saigon) becomes a French colony; Cambodia falls under French protection
1874	Annam in central Vietnam becomes a French protectorate
1885	Tonkin in the north of Vietnam becomes a French protectorate
1893	Laos falls under French protection
1930	Ho Chi Minh founds the Vietnamese Communist Party; renamed the Indochinese Communist Party to spur revolution throughout Indochina
June 1940	France surrenders to Nazi Germany; Vichy government assumes administration of Indochina
September 1940	Japan occupies Indochina; joint administration with Vichy government
March 1945	Japanese troops seize direct control of Indochina; French officials imprisoned or executed
September 1945	Japan signs terms of surrender; Ho Chi Minh proclaims Democratic Republic of Vietnam in the north
1945–46	French and allied forces reoccupy Indochina
December 1947	Fighting breaks out in Hanoi between French and Viet Minh forces signaling start of First Indochina War
1949	Elysée Accords establish Associated States within the French Union of Indochina. State of Vietnam in the south, Cambodia, and Laos granted internal autonomy, but foreign relations and defense under French control
May 1950	Start of American military and economic assistance to French and Associated States forces battling communist insurgents
September–October 1950	French forces in Tonkin suffer defeat at the hands of the Viet Minh in battles along the Chinese border
January–May 1951	Viet Minh are repulsed during series of attacks against the De Lattre Line protecting Hanoi and the Red River Delta
April 1953	Viet Minh invasion of Laos; royal capital at Luang Prabang threatened
March–May 1954	Battle of Dien Bien Phu; French suffer catastrophic defeat
April–July 1954	Geneva Conference talks aimed at ending the war
July 21, 1954	Geneva Peace Accords signed; Laos gains independence

theater in an effort to crush the Viet Minh insurgency and salvage the honor of France. In the end, some 110,000 French and local French Union soldiers would be lost in the attempt.[1]

More significantly for the region, what had started out as a simple campaign of French colonial re-conquest and restoration of global prestige had morphed into a major Cold War confrontation that would likely determine the future fate of region, and possibly of Western security, for decades to come.

Following Mao Zedong's victory over his Chinese Nationalist foes in 1949, Peking turned its attention toward actively assisting its Viet Minh communist brethren in their struggle against the French. In addition to providing critical rear bases and training for Ho's forces, the Chinese also provided tons of weapons and equipment, assigned hundreds of Chinese military advisers to Viet Minh combat units, and kept up a steady stream of supplies flowing across the border into northern Tonkin.[2] This assistance not only began to transform the nature of the war in Indochina, given the ability of the Viet Minh to go toe to toe with French Union forces, but it would force a likeminded American escalation in aid and rising U.S. military involvement in the region.

The outbreak of the Korean War in June 1950, followed by direct Chinese intervention in that conflict, vividly underscored the frailty of Asian security. It also energized the United States to go all out in its support of its Western ally in Indochina. American military equipment and supplies, from aircraft and tanks to ammunition and medicine began to flood into Indochina, creating an assistance program that was second only to support for U.S. combat troops in Korea.[3] All this would come at a steep price. This internationalization of the Indochina conflict would not only change the nature of the warfare, but increasingly give Washington a greater say in the final outcome of the war. But then again, Paris had little choice: the war was going badly and it desperately needed the Americans' help.

Although this massive assistance—$342 million in 1953 congressional appropriations alone[4]—and other changes within the French military hierarchy and structure in Indochina bought time, underlying political problems and an ineffective counterinsurgency strategy failed to reverse the tide of war. Moreover, the French had failed not only to stem the Viet Minh advance, but they had now ceded the battlefield initiative to the enemy. Domestic political pressure was also building in France by 1954 to negotiate an end to the war. Time was clearly running out and the collapse of French Indochina was a distinct possibility.

This sent alarm bells ringing in Washington with American security officials warning of the most severe consequences, including "the establishment of Communist control over Indochina ... that would almost certainly result in the Communization of all of Southeast Asia."[5] This new sense of urgency pushed U.S. military planners to consider a post-French Indochina strategy, one that was designed to prevent the countries of region from passing into the communist orbit by strengthening the ability of independent Indochinese states to politically and militarily resist communist-backed aggression. Central to this effort would be American aid directed at

The Battle For Laos: Vietnam's Proxy War 1955–1975

The Japanese occupation of French Indochina during World War II signaled the death knell of French colonialism and fueled the rise of nationalism and demands for self-determination.

developing indigenous forces to provide for their own security. It would be this focus that would come to define American engagement in Laos for the next two decades.

The growing U.S. concern over the future of French Indochina was well founded. By early 1954 the eyes of the world were trained on the besieged French garrison at Dien Bien Phu in what was shaping up to be the decisive battle of the war. In the run-up to the battle, General Vo Nguyen Giap's forces struck vital communication lines between Hanoi and

The French Defense of Laos

Strategically insignificant with regard to the military struggle between Viet Minh and French Union forces that was being played out elsewhere in Indochina, especially in neighboring Tonkin and the north's Red River Delta, Laos remained an isolated and neglected backwater for most of the war. Thus, the defense of the country was left to a handful of regular French units intermingled with colonial troops and elements of the newly constituted Lao National Army. These forces exercised de facto control over the country by occupying major towns and cities and manning a loose collection of defensive outposts spread across the countryside. Sporadic fighting against Viet Minh irregulars and their Pathet Lao allies was generally limited to countering small-scale attacks, hit-and-run raids, ambushes, and skirmishing.

All this would begin to change in the late autumn of 1952 as Laos assumed new importance in both the Viet Minh and French calculus.

Following a series of military setbacks in the Red River Delta, General Vo Nguyen Giap redirected his attention to the mountainous and dense jungle region of northwestern Tonkin near the border with Laos. It was part of his plan to engage the French on more favorable terrain and force them to divert resources from the defense of Hanoi and the Red River Delta. Moreover, from this location Giap could also mount an invasion into weakly defended Laos, which would further stretch French forces and burnish the image of the Pathet Lao insurgency. Thus, even as the fighting escalated in western Tonkin, some of Giap's forces crossed the Ma River into northeast Laos and launched a series of harassing attacks against French and Lao units near the town of Sam Neua.

The real test, however, would come in early 1953 when thousands of Viet Minh soldiers crossed the frontier into northern Laos at Sop Nao and linked up with Pathet Lao fighters. With the notable exception of the heroic garrison at Muong-Khoua, the feeble French defenses quickly collapsed in the face of this onslaught: outposts were overrun, units disintegrated, and columns of civilians and soldiers streamed southward. By late April the royal capital at Luang Prabang was nearly encircled and the remaining French strongpoints on the Plain of Jars were isolated and in danger of falling. Despite this deteriorating military situation, King Sisavang Vong refused to abandon the royal capital and French treaty obligations forced Paris to come to his aid. Fortunately, the early onset of monsoon rains and the timely arrival of French reinforcements—including artillery and strike aircraft—stymied the communist offensive by early May. Shortly thereafter, General Giap began withdrawing his forces to the north of the country satisfied that he had accomplished his objectives of diverting French forces away from Tonkin, shoring up the Pathet Lao's infrastructure in the northeast, and laying the groundwork for future incursions.

While the direct threat to Laotian security had abated, the long-term political and military implications of this offensive would be highly significant in influencing French war strategy in the coming year. For the Americans the near loss of Laos to the communists resulted in Washington increasing the pressure on Paris to abandon its defensive mindset and aggressively go over to the offensive in 1954/5. For the French high command in Indochina it meant reoccupying the old frontier outpost of Dien Bien Phu to thwart future attacks into Laos and hopefully lure Giap's forces into a decisive set-piece battle, one where the Viet Minh would be overwhelmed by French firepower. Another incursion into northeastern Laos by six Viet Minh battalions on Christmas Day 1953, as well as the Viet Minh seizure of Thakhek on the Mekong River in the panhandle also served to underscore the French need for urgency in bringing Giap's forces to heel.

Although the decisive battle of the Indochina War would be fought not on Laotian soil, but across the border at Dien Bien Phu from March to May 1954, the ramifications of that war and the terms of the resulting peace settlement would ultimately draw the country into an ever-widening Cold War conflict that would engulf the Lao people for the next 20 years.

The Battle For Laos: Vietnam's Proxy War 1955–1975

President Harry Truman was forced to balance the conflicting geopolitical demands of supporting the French political need to restore its colonial empire in Southeast Asia against his own wartime pledge to promote democracy and freedom around the world. (Photo U.S. National Archives)

Haiphong and the main French airfields in the Red River Delta. Meanwhile, Viet Minh irregulars launched guerrilla attacks in the far south of the Vietnamese peninsula and still other Viet Minh forces launched incursions into Laos to divert French forces. In mid-March the assault on Dien Bien Phu began with the northern positions being overrun in a matter of days. The writing was on the wall. Ultimately, the capitulation of the garrison in early May 1954 after a bloody 56-day siege and the formal signing of the Geneva Peace Accords on July 21, 1954 would be the closing act for French Indochina.

While the fighting had come to an end for now, the Cold War adversaries and their surrogates were preparing for the next round. The French were out, but the Americans were just getting started. It would be a journey that would pull them ever deeper toward a second Indochina war. While the growing American military involvement in South Vietnam would soon take center stage and occupy the public's attention by the mid-1960s, a far quieter, yet critical U.S. military involvement in Laos had long been underway.

An Uneasy Peace

The 1954 Geneva agreement officially brought an end to the fighting and with it peace in Indochina. Laos became a fully independent state under a constitutional monarchy. It all seemed worth it. Yet finding peace for the Vietnamese people and their Khmer and Lao neighbors would prove to be as elusive as ever in the years following the signing of the accords. This would be especially true for the Laotian people, who would find themselves plunged into a civil war within five years; the battle for Laos was just beginning.

But in July 1954 there was still hope for peace. The immediate post-World War II experience in Laos had shown that coalition governments were possible, even if somewhat chaotic. There was respect for the King Sisavang Vong, who tried to remain above the political fray, and there appeared to be a sincere desire to achieve some form of national reconciliation. There was also strong sentiment to avoid choosing sides in the superpower contest as Lao neutrality seemed highly prized, even if unrealistic to most observers. Still the road ahead would be difficult and the political machinations of the Cold War unavoidable as Laos struggled to find its place in a post-French Indochina world.

Talks between the government of Prince Souvanna Phouma and the North Vietnamese-allied Pathet Lao got underway in January 1955 over the latter's relinquishing control over the northeastern provinces of Phong Saly and Sam Neua as stipulated under the terms of the Geneva accords. This task, however, was complicated by the continuing presence of North Vietnamese advisers—in violation of the peace agreement—and the development of a parallel Pathet Lao administration of the area. The introduction of government troops to key towns in the northeast only served to heighten tensions and the talks collapsed by April; they resumed again in the summer only to collapse again in September.

In the meantime, the country headed toward its first post-independence general elections in December 1955 amid the unstable environment. Not unexpectedly the elections were boycotted by the Pathet Lao and no voting took place in the northeast given the ongoing territorial dispute. Moreover, none of the contesting political parties was able to gain a parliamentary majority, so Prince Souvanna was once again tapped to be prime minister. Committed to reconciliation, Souvanna was able to persuade his older half-brother, Prince Souphanouvong, the Pathet Lao leader, to return to negotiations in August 1956. By December a deal was in hand. Their agreement called for an immediate ceasefire to the sporadic fighting, plans to conduct a supplemental election (so the Pathet Lao could contest legislative seats), and the creation of a coalition government.[6]

U.S. General Joseph Collins (left center) arrives in Hanoi to inspect American military aid and assess strategy for countering the Viet Minh insurgency with General Lattre de Tassigny, commander of French forces, October 1951. (Photo Museum of the U.S. Air Force)

The Battle For Laos: Vietnam's Proxy War 1955–1975

Ho Chi Minh, the face of Vietnamese nationalism, would become a constant thorn in the side of first the French and then the Americans.

Nonetheless, tensions persisted. Lingering suspicions, personal animosities, and deep-seated ideological divisions hampered efforts to achieve peace and true national reconciliation. While a broad coalition government that included the Pathet Lao had been established, there continued to be problems bringing the northeastern provinces under central government control and Pathet Lao demands hindered the formation of a new, integrated national army. In point of fact, Hanoi's strategy of building up a core of Pathet Lao political and military cadre in North Vietnam continued unabated. Against this backdrop the long-awaited supplemental elections took place in May 1958 with the Laotian Patriotic Front (LPF), the newly organized Pathet Lao political party, capturing nearly two-thirds of the 21 legislative seats available. The Laotian Patriotic Front gains combined with disaffected independents and so-called "neutralists" precipitated a political crisis by denying Souvanna the premiership.

In an attempt to revive his fortunes, Souvanna joined forces with several conservative groups "to unite the nationalists' forces for the resolute fight against Communism and subversion."[7] It would be too little too late. Souvanna's failure to take a harder line with Souphanouvong and the Pathet Lao, as well as deepening American concern over rampant governmental corruption led to the suspension of all U.S. economic assistance. Souvanna was out. In his place a new right-wing, anti-communist government was installed in mid-August with American blessing.[8] This, increasingly Western-aligned, government quickly repudiated any efforts at reconciliation with the communist Pathet Lao. Once again war clouds were building.

Foreign Intervention: A Slippery Slope

Laos's domestic challenges in the late 1950s were further compounded by rising foreign meddling, both from East and West. Over the course of time the thin veneer of Laotian neutrality as enshrined in the Geneva peace accords would steadily give way to an ever-escalating war, albeit one fought in the shadows, between North Vietnam and its Pathet Lao allies and the United States and the government forces of Laos and Thailand. This seemingly inevitable slide toward war was well underway even prior to the collapse of the Souvanna government in 1958 as both Washington and Hanoi sought to advance their own agendas in Laos.

Eager to strengthen newly independent Laos as a critical buffer against the spread of communism, the Eisenhower administration initiated a large-scale economic and security assistance program. Between 1955 and 1958 Washington would send more than $200 million to the Laotian government.[9] The influx of this American aid—the largest in terms of per capita received at that time—would also soon swamp the tiny economy, create strong inflationary pressure, and open the door to extensive graft and corruption.[10] Most critically, very little of this aid would find its way to impoverished rural Lao communities where it would do the most good to shore up support for the central government. Thus, significant elements of the society would remain largely detached and alienated from the political elites in Vientiane, who were claiming to be building a united and prosperous country for all.

Security assistance was a central component of the American effort from the onset with some $34 million being allocated in January 1955 to modernize the Lao military.[11] Washington's desire to train and equip a force capable of ensuring domestic security in the face of the Pathet Lao threat, however, was complicated by the terms of the Geneva accords that only permitted the presence of a small French training mission in the country. To circumvent this restriction the United States established the Programs Evaluation Office (PEO), ostensibly as part of the U.S. Agency for International Development, in December 1955 as a tool for funneling security assistance directly to the Lao military. In reality the PEO was a disguised American military assistance mission, staffed by retired or active duty U.S. military personnel removed from U.S. Department of Defense rolls and tasked with assisting the French in training the roughly 23,000-man Royal Lao Army. The PEO, however, soon took on a life of its own, funding Lao army salaries, providing equipment and training, and even in assisting the shuttling of arms to anti-communist guerrillas in the mountainous eastern regions of the country. By late 1958 the Americans had completely supplanted the French training mission with the PEO expanding from a few dozen advisers to some 150 Special Forces personnel on temporary duty, plus an additional 100 Filipino military veterans employed by a newly formed front company,[12] to create an American advisory presence on par with that in South Vietnam.

Given the primitive road network, difficult mountainous terrain, and poor communications infrastructure, the development of an effective air component to facilitate the distribution of U.S. military assistance was essential. This role would be filled by contract pilots and support staff of Civil Air Transport (CAT) under the control of the U.S. mission in Vientiane. Based out of neighboring Udorn, Thailand, the airline's

C-46 and C-47 transports began delivering food, ammunition, and weapons, as well as airlifting troops to far-flung government outposts in late 1956. CAT established a permanent presence in Vientiane and would change its name to Air America in March 1959.[13] As a proprietary airline of the CIA, Air America would evolve into a key component of the Agency's secret war in Laos during the 1960s and 1970s.

This growing American entanglement in Laotian security affairs dramatically raised the political stakes for the Eisenhower administration in Southeast Asia by increasing tying the fate of the country to the coming U.S.-led confrontation with the forces of international communism. The Americans, however, were not alone in militarizing the situation as Hanoi was loath to abandon the strategic gains it had made in Laos during the First Indochina War. And just like the Americans, the North Vietnamese were keen to not only secure their foothold in northeastern Laos, but to expand their presence and influence across the country. For while the Pathet Lao and the LPF were the official face of popular communist resistance to the Vientiane government, there was little doubt that Hanoi was calling the shots.

Despite the official withdrawal of all Viet Minh units following the 1954 Geneva accords, hundreds of North Vietnamese soldiers secretly remained behind in Laos to provide training, advising, and logistics support to Pathet Lao forces in their northeast stronghold. In addition, thousands more "Vietnamese volunteers" directly under Hanoi's control also began regularly operating in central and southern Laos. A key priority for

American B-26 bomber repainted in French colors as part of the billions of dollars in U.S. military aid and equipment provided to French forces in Indochina between 1950 and 1954. (Photo U.S. Air Force)

The Land of A Million Elephants

Above left: Prince Souvanna's efforts to steer a non-aligned course and preserve the neutrality of Laos clashed with the harsh reality of rising superpower competition in the region.

Above right: Prince Souphanouvong, the public face of the communist Pathet Lao, was an ardent disciple of Ho Chi Minh's.

them was to expand the operational reach of communist forces in the country and support the expansion of the Pathet Lao forces, which in 1958 only numbered about 2,000 men under arms. To support this effort, Hanoi put in place a small, yet highly efficient network for funneling supplies and equipment across the Laotian frontier.

To further strengthen its grip on Laos, Hanoi worked diligently to develop a new generation of handpicked military and political leadership to do its bidding. It set up a training center and officer candidate school in Son Tay, North Vietnam, to groom a loyal set of Lao cadres. It also used educational inducements and offers of specialized training to help boost recruiting into the Pathet Lao ranks. In addition, North Vietnamese political cadres began working to build indigenous Lao support among the highland tribes along the eastern border, a task greatly simplified by the strong historic and familial ties that extended across the Lao–Vietnamese border. Significantly, this rising foothold in eastern Laos would return long-term strategic benefits as it allowed Hanoi to lay the foundation for clandestinely moving men and supplies across southern Laos into South Vietnam and Cambodia, a logistics and supply network that would better become known in the years ahead as the Ho Chi Minh Trail.

Thus, the stage was set for the coming conflict in Laos, one that while rooted in domestic divisions, would find itself increasingly engulfed in the larger building East–West confrontation over the future of the Vietnamese peninsula. And while the Vietnam War would come to define the United States and an entire generation for decades to come, another high-stakes struggle in Laos would be played out in the shadows, one largely out of sight and out of mind of the American people.

2. A NATION DIVIDED

The collapse of the Souvanna government would prove to be a defining point. In retrospect it ended all hope of national reconciliation and placed the country squarely on the road to political chaos and civil war. It was also perhaps inevitable that such a new and fragile country with deep-seated internal social and political divisions would be unable to weather the coming storm. Moreover, Laos was now well on its way to becoming simply a pawn in a greater confrontation that would soon envelope nearly all of Southeast Asia.

Not that the outside forces had much of master plan for Laos either. Much of what would play out between the United States and its Western allies and North Vietnam and its communist supporters was an ad hoc and improvised response to each escalating domestic crisis. This, however, would fuel foreign policy actions that were opportunistic at best and ill-conceived and poorly thought out at worse. Ironically, even as both sides saw deescalation in Laos as in their longer-term strategic interests, their very actions ultimately turned the country into a turbulent battlefield for the next decade and a half.

A Building Storm

Following the ouster of the Souvanna government in August 1958, a protracted period of instability and uncertainty ensued as various Lao factions jockeyed for power and courted external allies for support. This increasingly pushed conservative Lao political leaders to the right and to assume a more outright anti-communist and pro-Western stance to secure vital support from the United States and its regional allies. It also burnished the influence of rightwing elements within the military and indirectly encouraged them to take a more activist role in politics. Thus finding themselves increasingly disenfranchised from the Lao political system, the neutralists and the Pathet Lao factions turned to the Soviet Union, China, and North Vietnam to counter rising Western influence, which then precipitated a reactive cycle of further West intervention. Ultimately this growing polarization left little room for compromise, let alone peaceful reconciliation.

King Savang Vatthana, last King of Laos (1959–1975).

The political crisis was further aggravated in May 1959 when ongoing efforts to integrate

In a bid to avoid all-out civil war, competing Lao political factions repeatedly turned to government by coalition as a solution; all ended in failure. From left: Prince Souvanna (neutralists), Prince Boum Oum (rightists), and Prince Souphanouvong (communists).

Pathet Lao forces into the Lao National Army collapsed over the terms of the integration. One of the two Pathet Lao battalions then deserted to the northeast, crossing over the border into North Vietnam to seek sanctuary. In Vientiane, Prince Souphanouvong and other Pathet Lao leaders were quickly placed under house arrest. By mid-July sporadic fighting between government and Pathet Lao forces broke out in Phong Saly and Sam Neua provinces and numerous government outposts were abandoned. Soon the Lao army garrison at Sam Neua was isolated and completely dependent on air resupply. Rumors also began to circulate that hordes of Pathet Lao and North Vietnamese troops were preparing to march on Vientiane.

The deteriorating situation caused panic in Washington. In response, the Americans quickly announced an emergency expansion of their military training program in Laos—using U.S. Special Forces advisers—and dispatched additional equipment, including tanks, trucks, and transport aircraft, in the hope of containing the crisis in the northeast.[1] It also precipitated the Joint Chiefs of Staff to update their contingency plans for direct U.S. military intervention in Laos. Despite serious concerns over potential Chinese reaction to a potential American military presence on its border, President Dwight Eisenhower approved the plan and U.S. forces in the Pacific were put on alert in early September and ready to move. The United States was increasingly moving to a war footing in Southeast Asia.

Fortunately, at the behest of Vientiane government the United Nations stepped in to defuse the situation. By October 1959 tensions had abated as all sides pulled back from the brink. The death of King Sisavang Vong in late October and the pending succession of his son, Savang Vatthana, also contributed to the political uncertainty as the various Lao factions and their external supporters reassessed their positions. While full-scale war had been adverted for the time being, the stark political divide within Lao society and the willingness, even recklessness, of the United States and North Vietnam to engage in military brinkmanship set the stage for the coming conflict.

Any respite would be short-lived, however, as Brigadier General Phoumi Nosavan's rightist coup d'état at the end of December brought in a feeble provisional government in the run-up to the April 24, 1960 National Assembly elections. Under the watchful eye of the military, electoral districts were gerrymandered, communist-aligned candidates disqualified, and the vote count brazenly manipulated to ensure an overwhelming, conservative and pro-military victory.

In the faint hope of tempering conservative elements, King Savang appointed a moderate, Prince Tiao Somsanith (who was also former Prime Minister Souvanna's nephew), as head of the new government. General Phoumi, however, stayed on as Minister of Defense, while other rightwing politicians were installed in senior government positions. It was clear who was running the country; no quarter would be given to the communists.

Fighting Resumes

That fighting would resume was a foregone conclusion following the rigged April 1960 elections and the new military-aligned government's crackdown on the opposition. Neither side would have to wait long as Phoumi's intention to prosecute Prince Souphanouvong for subversive activities provided the catalyst. Forewarned, Souphanouvong and other imprisoned Pathet Lao leaders were able to escape their Vientiane cells on May 23 and make their way northeast to Sam Neua, where they were warmly received by their supporters. Shortly thereafter, low-level skirmishing between Pathet Lao and government forces broke out as the communists maneuvered to strengthen their grip over key eastern portions of the country. In hindsight the conflict spreading to the south of the country signaled a significant watershed in the civil war and one with serious future implications for both the United States and North Vietnam.

A year previous and after contentious debate, the North Vietnamese leadership committed itself "to the overthrow of the Diem government [in Saigon] through not only political agitation but also through military means"[2] and initiated a long-term plan to increase direct aid for the liberation of South Vietnam. In support of this effort, Hanoi created a Special Military Operations Corps, known as "Group 559" (named after its founding in May 1959), to build and maintain an extensive logistical supply route that ran through the panhandle of eastern Laos along the nearly 700-mile-long Annamese cordillera mountain range into South Vietnam.[3] The Americans would soon label it the Ho Chi Minh Trail.

This undertaking would not only require a massive commitment of men and equipment to traverse the challenging terrain of mountains, rivers, and jungle forests of southeastern Laos, but it needed to be hidden from the prying eyes of the Americans and their allies. As such the North Vietnamese worked with the Pathet Lao to sway local hill tribes to their side and undermine government control over the eastern portions of Khammouan

A Nation Divided

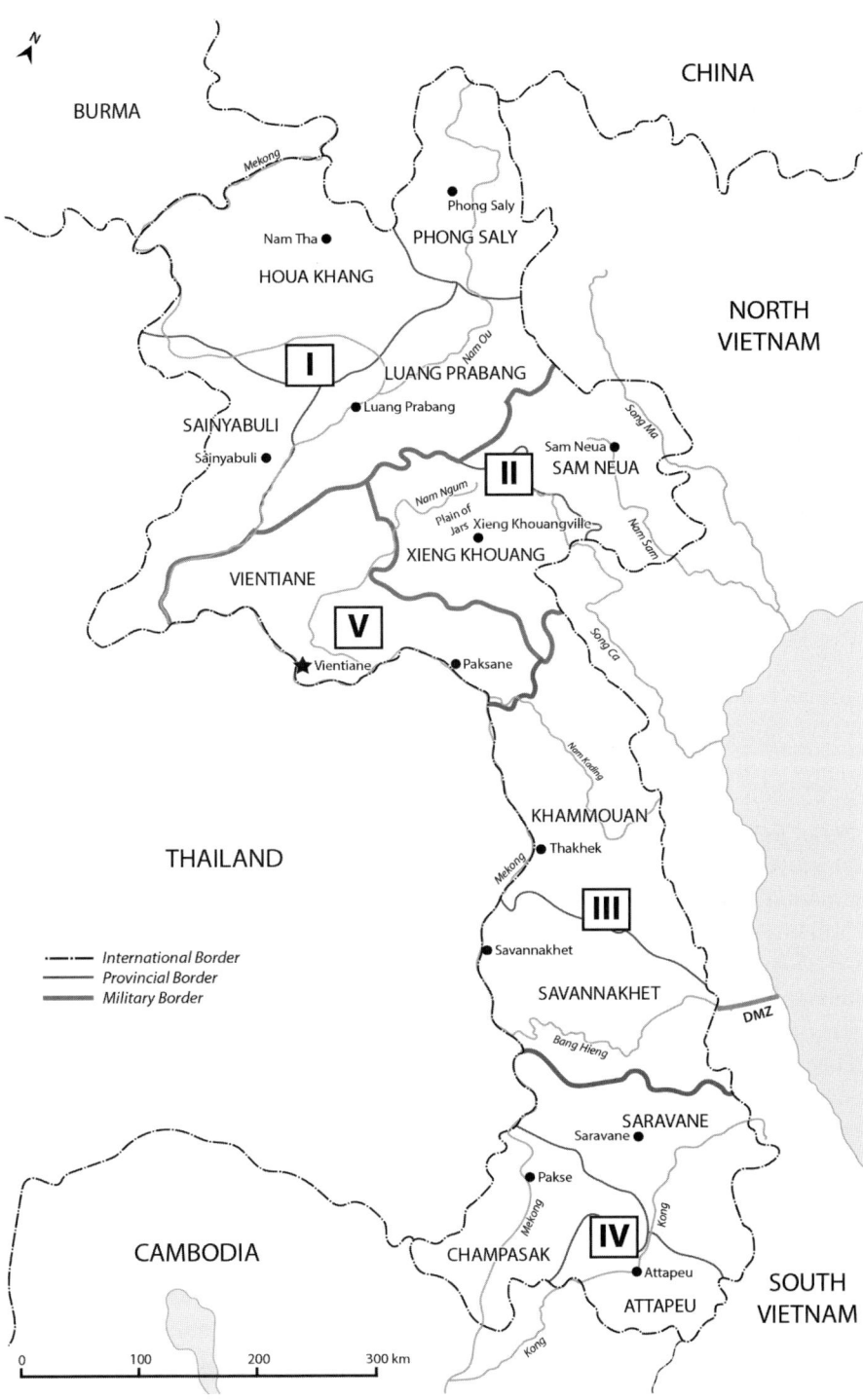

Laotian Theater.

The Battle For Laos: Vietnam's Proxy War 1955-1975

and Savannakhet provinces bordering North Vietnam. This not only expanded Pathet Lao influence outside the northeast, but would provide a fertile recruiting ground for swelling their ranks.

To counter this communist buildup in the panhandle, the Vientiane government dispatched a number of troops, including those of the elite 2nd Parachute Battalion, to reestablish control. Commanding the 2nd Parachute Battalion was a 26-year-old captain, Kong Le. At barely five feet tall with a wiry frame, he was not an imposing figure, yet he had proven himself to be an excellent field commander and commanded the respect and loyalty of his men.[4] Shortly after returning to the capital in early August following its extended deployment, the 2nd Parachute Battalion was ordered back into the field to clear pockets of Pathet Lao troops north of Vientiane. This proved to be a breaking point for Kong Le and his men.

U.S. Special Forces instructors sought to mold the nascent Lao national army into an effective counterweight to communist Pathet Lao forces. (Photo Museum of the U.S. Air Force)

Weary of the political infighting, rampant government corruption, and fruitless operational deployments, Kong Le launched a coup d'état on August 9, 1960 while most senior government officials were away in the royal capital of Luang Prabang. His paratroopers faced little resistance and quickly gained control of the airport and other key installations across the Vientiane. In announcing the formation of a new Neutralist government, Kong Le underscored his desire to bring about an end to the fighting, stem corruption, and end foreign interference in the country. He also insisted that the new government would return Laos "to a 'policy of genuine neutrality,' [one that] would allow the country to avoid being overpowered by foreign influences."[5] In doing so, Kong Le tapped into widespread discontent among the average Laotian and he was widely seen a heroic figure. At Kong Le's urging Souvanna was picked to form a new government by King Savang on August 16.

Unwilling to accept their loss of power, General Phoumi and other rightwing elements formed an alternative government headed by Prince Boun Oum. From their base in Savannakhet in southeast Laos, Phoumi and Boun Oum encouraged the Thai government to impose an economic blockade of Vientiane and began making plans to retake the capital. For its part, the United States found itself caught up in the middle of this power struggle and adopted a wait-and-see attitude that alienated all sides. Relations between the Souvanna government and Washington, however, worsened further following the Neutralists' overtures to the Pathet Lao concerning the formation of a coalition government, the continuing American suspension of economic aid, and the U.S. failure to overturn the Thai blockade. Not surprisingly, Souvanna then turned to the Soviet Union and China for assistance. In November, Moscow agreed to help and began airlifting arms, fuel, and supplies into Laos to shore up the Neutralist government. Thus rather than defuse tensions, Le Kong's coup had ironically once again stoked the fires of a superpower competition in Laos.

In late November, General Phoumi's forces—now with American and Thai advisers and logistics support—began its march up National Route 13 to wrest back control of Vientiane. Honoring their pledge to assist Souvanna, the Soviets in the first two weeks of December flew at least 34 military resupply flights, including the uplifting of a complete North Vietnamese heavy artillery battery and crew, into the capital.[6] The battle for Vientiane was joined on December 13 when troops under the command of Colonel Kouprasith Abhay, the city's southern garrison commander and now aligned with General Phoumi, attacked Kong Le's forces. Although Kouprasith's men were initially repelled by Kong Le's paratroopers, the attackers were soon reinforced by Phoumi's heavily armed column that included tanks and artillery. Fighting continued into December 16, with artillery duels crisscrossing the city skies, until the outnumbered and outgunned Neutralist troops were forced to retreat northward. Although casualties were relatively light for the opposing forces, more than 500 civilians were killed or injured during the fighting.[7]

Kong Le's forces fell back north along National Route 13 to Vang Vieng, some 55 miles from the capital, where at this point Soviet IL-14 transports airlifted Kong Le and his men to the southern edge of the Plain of Jars. Linking up with Pathet Lao forces in the area and assisted by a massive Soviet air bridge that flew 184 sorties into Laos from Hanoi between mid-December and early January 1961,[8] the newly resupplied and rearmed joint force then moved to drive troops aligned with Phoumi off their positions on the plain. This offensive in conjunction with a North Vietnamese-led assault—complete with tanks and heavy artillery—on the key crossroads at Ban Ban on the far eastern edge of the Plain of Jars in late December threated to turn the tide of the war against Phoumi and Boun Oum.

Outgunned and outnumbered, panic set in among the rightist troops in the face of this concerted attack. Soldiers abandoned their positions and fled, while their tribal allies retreated to the nearby mountaintops. Khang Khay quickly fell, as did the provincial capital of Xieng Khouangville as the North Vietnamese column methodically advanced down National Route 7. By early January 1961 the Neutralists-Pathet Lao coalition could claim, thanks in large part to the Soviet and North Vietnamese military assistance, control over every strategic road junction on the Plain of Jars.[9]

War had come to Laos and the United States and its regional allies were finding themselves increasing dragged into a growing Cold War military confrontation, because of Washington's and Moscow's staunch determination to support their respective Lao proxies in a fight that in reality held little geostrategic importance for either superpower.

The new incoming administration of President John F. Kennedy found itself facing a major crisis in Laos. Having the country fall to the forces of international communism would result, according the U.S. intelligence community, in serious damage to

Lima Site 26, a typical unimproved dirt airstrip, located in the far western part of Xieng Khouang Province, 1965. (Photo Museum of the U.S. Air Force)

American creditability in Southeast Asia. Laos was becoming "a symbolic test of intentions, wills, and strengths between the major powers of the West and the Communist bloc."[10] Nonetheless, Kennedy was reluctant to risk sending in American troops if there was any way around it. Besides, such a provocative U.S. military action was likely to spur further North Vietnamese and Soviet involvement. It might even provoke direct Chinese military intervention and no one in the Kennedy administration wanted a replay of the Korean War. Thus, Kennedy's challenge was, according to senior adviser Walt Rostow, "to convince the communists that he would, in fact, fight if necessary to avoid a communist takeover while seeking a political settlement."[11]

While Washington struggled to find a solution that walked this fine line, the fighting continued. An airborne government assault on Xieng Khouangville failed to dislodge Kong Le's forces there and the attackers were forced to retreat. American airdrops of small arms and ammunition to tribal Hmong irregulars aligned with the Boun Oum government helped stiffen resistance in the mountains surrounding the plain, but these brave yet poorly equipped and trained troops had little hope of resisting any sustained attacks by the more heavily armed communist forces. Not unexpectedly, Hmong mountaintop bases at Khang Kho and San Tiau were overrun by March. Intense fighting also continued along National Route 13 linking Vientiane to Luang Prabang as General Phoumi's men struggled to keep their lines of communication open. Meanwhile, the government garrison at Sam Neua in the heart of Pathet Lao country fell under siege and became entirely dependent on aerial resupply for its survival.

A Nation Divided

The Swiss-made PC-6 Porter was a short take-off and landing aircraft particularly well-suited for the country's rugged and improvised runways.

To the south in Khammouan Province, North Vietnamese and Pathet Lao troops ousted Phoumi's troops from much of the area north and east of the Nam Theum and Ca Dinh rivers. The important crossroads of Lak Sao fell on April 11, as did the key towns of Muong Phine and Tchepone to elements of Hanoi's 325th Division.[12] The communist advance down National Route 9 pushed Phoumi's troops back to Moung Pha Lan and allowed Group 559 to realign its supply lines to the western side of the Annamite Mountains. Engineers from the 325th Division also repaired the airfield at Tchepone, enabling the creation of the first North Vietnamese forward operating airfield in southern Laos.[13] The communists were well on their way to solidifying their grip on this critical part of the panhandle.

Giving Diplomacy a Chance

The approaching rainy season and growing war weariness on the part of the combatants opened the door for a ceasefire in May 1961, which was also welcomed by both Washington and Moscow. Following a flurry of diplomatic activity, it was agreed to reactivate the 1954 Geneva Conference's International Control Commission (ICC) as a prelude to a ceasefire beginning on May 11. Five days later 14 countries, including the United States, Soviet Union, China, and North Vietnam, convened a second Geneva conference aimed at diplomatically resolving the Laotian crisis and bringing a permanent end to the fighting. Signaling their resolve to defuse tensions, President Kennedy and Soviet Premier Nikita Khrushchev publicly "reaffirmed their support of a neutral and independent Laos chosen by the Laotians themselves, and of international agreements for insuring that neutrality and independence."[14] Perhaps, just perhaps, a peaceful resolution to this Cold War conflict was possible.

Lima Sites

A key factor in sustaining America's secret war in Laos was its ability to provide critical military support to remote and isolated Hmong guerrilla outposts and enclaves, many deep inside communist-held territory. Without aerial resupply in the form of Air America-piloted aircraft this would have been all but impossible to accomplish. Thus, considerable attention was given to the establishment of a series of crude airstrips—many craved out of hillsides or along mountainous ridgelines—to support this effort.

Early on as a contractor for the U.S. government in the 1950s, Air America set about designating all airstrips within the kingdom with a unique site number. By May 1964 the lexicon had evolved to identify improved runways with the symbol "L" or Lima followed by a unique number, e.g. Savannakhet was Lima 39 (L 39) and Luang Prabang was Lima 54 (L 54). Similarly, unimproved airstrips were given the "LS" label followed by a unique number, e.g. Ban Padong was LS 5, Lak Sao was LS 49, and Moung Soi was L 60. Thus, as new airstrips were established they followed the same naming conventions.

In tandem with the CIA's paramilitary buildup in the mid-1960s, the U.S. Air Force instituted a covert program to install a navigational radar system—Tactical Air Navigation or TACAN—across selected areas of the country to assist American aircraft operating in Laos, as well as in neighboring North Vietnam. The first two TACAN sites were installed near Saravane in southern Laos and on Skyline Ridge near Long Chieng in late 1965. The sites were manned and equipped by Air Force personnel serving in a "non-official capacity" and were frequently co-located with existing lima sites. Other TACAN sites, however, had to be newly established, often high atop mountains in very remote and inhospitable terrain with nothing more than a small dirt airstrip to link them to the outside world. Hmong troops typically provided security at all American TACAN sites.

One of the more famous lima sites was LS 85, built high atop the 5,800-foot peak of Phu Pha Thi in northeast Laos, deep within Pathet Lao territory and only 160 miles west of Hanoi. Staffed by a contingent of Air Force technicians working clandestinely, who rotated in and out of the site by Air America helicopters, their mission was to man a TACAN beacon and an advanced navigational radar system that provided data for U.S. aircraft striking targets in North Vietnam.

In all there were in excess of 400 lima sites established during the war, but not all of them were operational at the same time. The airstrip runways of dirt, clay or grass ranged in length from a mere 800 feet to more than 4,000 feet, although most averaged about 1,500 feet in length. Support facilities ranged wildly from a few crude shacks with a single simple transmitter to dozens of propose-built structures and sophisticated communications facilities. A specialized fleet of Air America short takeoff and landing aircraft and helicopters helped service these sites, some of which required pilots to have not only skill, but nerves of steel too.

The task at hand, however, would prove more difficult to accomplish than either side imagined. Less than six months into his administration, Kennedy was forced to walk a delicate foreign policy line. On the one hand he needed to show strong resolve in confronting global communist aggression, especially in the wake of the failed Bay of Pigs invasion in Cuba in April. Yet on the other hand, he wanted to avoid militarily entangling the United States in a conflict with few strategic benefits and enormous risks. "Laos," Kennedy wrote, "is a most inhospitable area in which to wage a campaign [with] the chances of eradicating the Communist position ... practically nil."[15] It made more sense to confront communist—and especially North Vietnamese—aggression on the Vietnamese peninsula where the strategic and operational landscape favored anti-communist forces and where the prospects of an American victory were much greater.[16]

This led to a U.S. foreign policy strategy of "neutralizing" Laos through political means rather than through force of American arms. With these marching orders in hand, veteran diplomat Averell Harriman and his team went to work hammering out an agreement in Geneva that was acceptable to the United States, its Cold War foes, and the Laotian combatants. The goal was to create a tripartite government in Laos that included communists, anti-communists, and Neutralist elements, a government that would reduce foreign influence and, moreover, one that would allow Washington a face-saving public exit. It would be a long and arduous task and one taking more than a year to accomplish.

Meanwhile back in Laos the fighting went on despite the ceasefire as both sides sought to gain an advantage on the battlefield in the run-up to any peace settlement. While government forces concentrated on small-scale sweeps to eliminate pockets of enemy resistance in their territory, the Pathet Lao-Neutralist forces were especially keen to secure their grip on the strategic Plain of Jars. A major obstacle, however, to achieving this goal was the continuing presence of thousands of strident anti-communist Hmong fighters ensconced in mountain strongholds on the southern fringes of the plain. In mid-1961 the

Communist Pathet Lao forces would steadily strengthen their grip over northeast Laos throughout the early 1960s.

The Battle For Laos: Vietnam's Proxy War 1955–1975

The Viet Minh proved to be extremely innovative in utilizing any means available for transporting supplies through the Laotian panhandle to support the war in the South.

roughly 5,000 Hmong irregulars in the area were led by the charismatic and highly capable Lieutenant Colonel Vang Pao, a 31-year-old Hmong officer in the newly reconstituted Forces Armées du Royaume (Royal Armed Forces or FAR) of the Boun Oum government. (Vang Pao's relationship with CIA will be addressed in the next chapter.)

The Hmong were the principal ethnic minority of the Lao Soung (Lao of the mountain-tops) and the last major group to migrate from southern China in the early 19th century, settling mainly in the eastern mountainous regions of central Laos. Practicing slash-and-burn agriculture with opium as their principal cash crop, they maintained a strong sense of ethnic identity and tight clanship structure. As such they were often looked down on by the lowland Lao as savage, dirty, and drug-addicted people with a war-like mentality, best to be avoided. Many Hmong clans supplied guerrilla fighters to assist the French during the First Indochina War and suffered harsh reprisals from the Pathet Lao and North Vietnamese in that war's aftermath. Some Hmong clans, however, did align themselves with the communists in the 1950s and provided recruits to Pathet Lao ranks as well.[17]

By eliminating the Hmong strongholds adjacent to the plain, the Pathet Lao-Neutralist coalition would not only secure its grip, but also preempt the use of these bases as future launching pads for government counteroffensives. Accordingly, numerous so-called "police actions" were conducted to root out the Hmong fighters. Moung Ngai fell on May 12 and soon Vang Pao's main base at Padong, some 30 miles south of Khang Khay came under near constant artillery bombardment by North Vietnamese 75-mm howitzers. Despite repeated pleas to the ICC over these ongoing ceasefire violations, the

A Nation Divided

In late 1961 elements of the 45th Reconnaissance Squadron out of Misawa, Japan, were dispatched to Thailand to begin aerial monitoring the growing crisis in Laos.

bombardment continued. Despite determined resistance, Padong would be overrun and captured on June 7 following a full-scale infantry assault on the mountain base, but Vang Pao and most of his men and their families were able to escape capture.

While the onset of the rainy season from April to October put an end to most fighting, little progress was being made by Lao leaders over the composition of the proposed new coalition government. Although it was agreed that Souvanna would head the new government, the division of cabinet posts—particularly defense and interior—created a stumbling block. Boun Oum and General Phoumi were especially fearful of being out-maneuvered by the two half-brothers, Souvanna and Souphanouvong, and rejected any compromise. With the talks now deadlocked, Phoumi apparently sought to provoke a crisis by reinforcing the northwest provincial capital of Nam Tha with several thousand additional FAR troops in early February 1962. This would bring the size of the garrison there to about 5,000 men.[18]

Phoumi's apparent objective was to demonstrate that a military, rather than a political, solution was still possible. The result, however, was an unmitigated disaster. Phoumi's forces panicked in the face of a mounting Pathet Lao-North Vietnamese offensive against the garrison in early May. Nearly half his troops fled uncontrollably toward the Mekong River and into Thailand some 100 miles to the southeast and another 2,000 or so were captured along with large quantities of weapons and ammunition when Nam Tha fell.[19] In a show of force President Kennedy announced on May 15 the dispatch of some 3,000 American troops to the Thai–Lao border to demonstrate support for Boun Oum's government and head off any potential communist thrust toward Thailand. Thanks in part to Moscow's timely intervention with the Pathet Lao, the military threat subsided.

Now with his army thoroughly discredited, his negotiating position seriously weakened, and under growing American pressure, Boum Oum finally came to terms on the formation of a coalition government with Souvanna and Souphanouvong on June 11, 1962. Souvanna became prime minister and minister of defense, while Souphanouvong and Phoumi became deputy prime ministers. The majority of the cabinet posts were allotted to the Neutralists with the remainder split equally between the Pathet Lao and the rightists. Following the installation of the new tripartite government, foreign ministers attending the Geneva talks formally signed the Declaration and Protocol on the Neutrality of Laos in July and an early October deadline was given for the withdrawal of all foreign troops from Laotian soil. Laos officially—at least on paper—would no longer be a Cold War battlefield.

The Collapse of the Second Coalition

No one, however, was under the illusion that the new political agreements would bring immediate peace or signal a complete end to all foreign involvement, but Prime Minister Souvanna did his best to make things work. The final American military advisers were withdrawn from the country in October and the Soviets ended their airlifts, turning over several transport aircraft to the Souvanna government in December. Sporadic fighting died down and an uneasy truce continued to hold into 1963. Nonetheless, suspicions abounded among the three Lao factions and within their respective leaderships. Moreover, the country remained in a de facto state of partition, with the Neutralists, Pathet Lao, and rightists maintaining near exclusive control and authority over the territory their military forces occupied. In essence the central government held little real power and remained hostage to the whims and demands of its constituent parts.

U.S. Air Force RF-101s conducted some of the first clandestine aerial reconnaissance missions over Laos. (Photo Museum of the U.S. Air Force)

A Nation Divided

President John F. Kennedy meets with Prime Minister Souvanna at the White House in July 1962 at the height of the Laos crisis. (Photo JFK Presidential Library)

Not surprisingly, in April 1963, this house of cards collapsed. It seemed inevitable as tensions between the Pathet Lao and their former Neutralist partners had become increasingly strained. Since the end of the previous year Souphanouvong forces had been diverting the last of the Soviet airlifted supplies away from Kong Le's men. The shooting down of a government-chartered resupply flight to Kong Le by mutinous Neutralist troops and their subsequent defection to the Pathet Lao only further poured oil on the fire. The final straw came on April 1 when Foreign Minister Quinim Pholsena, a left-leaning Neutralist, was assassinated by a Kong Le supporter in retaliation for the previous killing of a close associate of Kong Le's and Souvanna's in February.[20] Following Quinim's death, the Pathet Lao leadership fled the capital for their headquarters at Khang Khay in Xieng Khouang Province. At the same time Kong Le decided to redeploy his remaining 4,000–5,000 loyal troops to the western Plain of Jars, where they linked up with Phoumi's FAR forces. This new joint force soon found itself under harassing artillery fire and infantry probes by Pathet Lao troops as the country once again teetered on the brink of open warfare.

Repeated attempts by Souvanna's to defuse the building crisis, including exploring the possibility of establishing a new demilitarized seat of government at Luang Prabang, failed to gain traction with Souphanouvong and the Pathet Lao leadership. Increasingly

Vang Pao, the Hmong leader and military commander of the CIA's secret army, would become the face of the anti-communist resistance in northern Laos.

confident of securing a military advantage, the communist forces in late January 1964 stepped up their attacks on both Kong Le's and Phoumi's forces. In an urgent effort to stop the fighting, Souvanna traveled to Peking and Hanoi in early April hoping to persuade the Chinese and North Vietnamese governments to pressure their Pathet Lao allies into a ceasefire.

Not only did Souvanna's gambit fail, but he soon found himself imprisoned following a rightist coup by generals Kouprasith Abhay and Siho Lamphoutacoul on April 19, 1964. Thanks, however, to strong diplomatic and economic pressure by the United States and other Western countries, Souvanna was quickly restored to power. But the damage was done. The hardline rightists were on the ascent. Phoumi was replaced as defense minister and plans were made to reorganize the FAR and merge it with Kong Le's forces into one single national army. Moreover, the de facto rightist takeover of the government and military caused Prince Souphanouvong officially to withdraw from the governing coalition in June. This effectively ended any hope of reaching a political solution as the middle ground had now completely evaporated.

Taking advantage of the political upheaval in Vientiane, as well as dissention and defections within the Neutralist ranks, Pathet Lao troops with North Vietnamese support launched a full-scale assault on May 16 against Kong Le's forces. Phoumi's demoralized FAR troops were unable to provide any meaningful assistance to their allies, thus leaving Kong Le's men to their fate and they were soon fighting for their lives. Beating a retreat westward to the town of Muong Soui that lay astride National Route 7 on the edge of the plain, they regrouped and organized their defenses. However, with reports of Pathet Lao forces pushing on toward the key road junction town of Sala Phou Khoum some 40 miles farther to the west, the Neutralist troops were in danger of being cut off completely.

A Navy RF-8A Crusader flying a Yankee Team reconnaissance mission over the Plain of Jars would become the first American military aircraft lost over Laos when it was shot down by antiaircraft fire on June 6, 1964. (Photo U.S. Navy)

This prompted Kong Le to call upon Prime Minister Souvanna for immediate air support to stem the enemy advance.

After a complicated diplomatic song and dance, the U.S. Embassy agreed to assist the nascent Royal Lao Air Force (RLAF)—which had more planes than trained pilots—in striking the Pathet Lao lines of supply. American-contract and Thai-piloted RLAF T-28 attack aircraft, armed with 100-pound and 500-pound bombs, also joined in on May 25 to supplement ongoing RLAF bombing missions.[21] Several days earlier, U.S. Air Force RF-101s based out of Thailand conducted the first American flights over the Plain of Jars as part of Yankee Team aerial reconnaissance missions, which provided a badly needed morale boost to the embattled Neutralists. In addition, the U.S. Embassy in Vientiane expedited the transfer of additional T-28s from the South Vietnamese Air Force to the Souvanna government, bringing the number of strike aircraft up to twenty.[22] During the first week in June, government and U.S.-contracted aircraft flew some 85 bombing sorties in support of Neutralist troops.[23] These air strikes along with the onset of the monsoon rains in June put an end to further attacks and Kong Le was able to maintain his grip on Muong Soui.

Of note too was the first loss of an American military aircraft over Laos when a Navy RF-8 Crusader off the USS *Kitty Hawk* was shot down by antiaircraft fire over Khang Khay while flying a Yankee Team mission on June 6. The pilot, Lieutenant Charles Klusmann, was captured, but managed to escape his captors with the help of fellow Lao prisoners in late August and return to active duty. This would be the first of almost 250 U.S. aircraft that would eventually be lost over Laos between 1964 and 1973.[24]

The Birth and Evolution of Air America

The origins of Air America—the secretly owned CIA airline that played such a vital role in the Agency's operations in Laos—can be traced back to August 1950 when the Central Intelligence Agency quietly purchased the assets of Civil Air Transport (CAT). The airline, which was started in China after World War II by General by Claire Chennault (of Flying Tigers fame) and Whiting Willauer, flew commercial routes across Asia and operated as a privately owned airline. At the same time, however, CAT Incorporated provided airplanes and crews for secret intelligence operations contracted by the U.S. government.

By mid-1956 CAT was becoming an instrumental part of U.S. military and humanitarian assistance programs in Laos by providing not only essential logistical support to the Laotian armed forces, but also in delivering emergency food relief to isolated districts and villages. The introduction of U.S. Special Forces training teams in the summer of 1959 further increased the demand for air transport services by the now-renamed Air America as part of Washington's efforts to stabilize the country and prevent a communist takeover.

With the Lao civil war now in full swing by 1961, the need to augment Air America's airlift capability was addressed by the transfer of 14 U.S. Marine UH-34 helicopters to Air America. In time, the rotary element of Air America would grow to some 30 helicopters, including large CH-47 Chinook cargo and troop-transport helicopters. This complemented another two dozen twin-engine fixed-wing transports, like the C-7, C-46, and C-123, as well as another two dozen smaller planes, including short-takeoff-and-landing aircraft such as the Pilatus PC-6 and Helio H-395 that were designed for servicing remote mountaintop airfields. By the early 1970s Air America could boast an inventory of nearly 80 aircraft and more than 300 pilots, mechanics, and air-freight specialists under its control.

From its main operating base at Udorn, Thailand, as well as from smaller airfields in Laos (lima sites) Air America planes and crew flew tens of thousands of missions ferrying troops, refugees, and supplies, as well as conducting photo-reconnaissance and emergency medevac missions, rescuing downed airmen, and inserting and extracting clandestine teams behind enemy lines. Most important of all, Air America aircraft were the logistics and communication lynchpin for supporting the CIA's secret army of Hmong fighters under General Vang Pao's command that often operated in far-flung and remote reaches of northern Laos, accessible only by air. As noted in the CIA's history, "Without Air America's presence, the CIA's effort in Laos could not have been sustained."

The end of America's war in Vietnam spelled an end to Air America. The last Air America aircraft left Laos in June 1974 and all operations in Thailand were terminated by the end of the month. The company finally closed down completely in June 1976, returning more than $20 million to the U.S. Treasury. And Air America faded into the history books.

(Source: W. Leary, "CIA Air Operations in Laos, 1955–1974.")

Part of Air America's fleet: a PC-6 Porter and a U-10D parked at Chiang Mai, Thailand. (Photo Museum of the U.S. Air Force).

In July and August FAR and Neutralist troops mounted a counteroffensive to shore up their position and recover critical territory. With the help of extensive RLAF air support, Operation Triangle was successful in ejecting Pathet Lao forces from the Sala Phou Khoum area, reopening National Route 13 northward to Luang Prabang, and restoring lines of communications to Kong Le's headquarters at Muong Soui. It also proved to be a major watershed for rising direct U.S. engagement in the war: Air America transport aircraft and helicopters airlifted men and supplies into the battlefield, U.S. jets flew tactical reconnaissance missions, and airborne American forward air controllers (FACs) helped direct RLAF and Thai-piloted T-28 air strikes against enemy targets.[25] Skirmishing also continued elsewhere along the northern and southern fringes of the Plain of Jars in the run-up to a new round of tripartite talks in September. The talks in Paris, however, failed to produce any new agreement or bring about an end to the fighting.

As 1964 drew to a close several important milestones had been reached and change was in the air, although what form this would take and what implications it would have for Laos were far from certain. The American effort to "neutralize Laos" and remove it as a venue for superpower competition had failed miserably and, despite Moscow's pullback, other regional communist powers were hell-bent on advancing their own agendas. The United States and its Thai allies countered this with the continued development and expansion of proxy forces, despite Washington's desire to keep the lid on the deepening conflict and out of the public limelight. Fate, however, had something different in store in the years ahead. Within the space of a few months in early 1965, the rapidly growing American involvement in neighboring South Vietnam and the start of a bombing campaign against North Vietnam would drag Laos even deeper into that war, a war that the country and its people would not be able to escape for another decade.

3. INTO THE VIETNAMESE QUAGMIRE

While the conflict in Laos continued to simmer along, entering its tenth year and still no closer to resolution, events in neighboring Vietnam were rapidly overshadowing the proxy war being waged across the Laotian landscape and skies. Once considered the lynchpin of Western security in Southeast Asia, the country would be pushed to the backburner of the East–West confrontation as escalating American military engagement in South Vietnam took center stage. In the space of a few short years, the United States would find itself involved in its largest military conflict since World War II, sending more than a half million men and massive amounts of military equipment into the fray.

Washington's Vietnamese Contagion

As much as it tried to avoid it, the administration of President Lyndon Johnson was becoming increasingly entangled in the Vietnamese conflict by 1965. As the de facto guarantor of South Vietnamese security following the French withdrawal from Indochina, the United States found itself in the unenviable position of trying to nurture the development of a democratic society and robust economy in South Vietnam as a bulwark

Secretary General Le Duan's unqualified support for the liberation struggle in the South put North Vietnam squarely on a collision course with the United States by 1964.

against communist aggression, while in the midst of a growing guerrilla insurgency that was threatening South Vietnam's continued survival as a nation. Ten years of American security assistance, training, and equipment to the Saigon government, as well as the presence of thousands of U.S. military advisers had failed to turn the tide. Moreover, Hanoi appeared firmly committed to supporting the Viet Cong insurgency by sending a steady stream of men and matériel southward—much of it through the Ho Chi Minh Trail in the Laotian panhandle.

Against this increasingly desperate backdrop, the Johnson administration sought to strengthen the Saigon government and provide it with a confidence boost, demonstrate American resolve in aiding its South Vietnamese ally, deter Hanoi from actively directing and supporting the Viet Cong insurgency, and push the North Vietnamese leadership toward peace negotiations. This, however, would be an uphill task. Setbacks on the battlefield, an unwieldy and unresponsive chain of command, and personal rivalries within the senior officer corps greatly hindered the effectiveness of the South Vietnamese military. Likewise, political intrigue and maneuvering by both civilian and military leaders complicated Washington's efforts to establish some degree of political stability in Saigon or build popular support for the government. Moreover, it was essential to persuade—or compel—Hanoi into ending its support to the Viet Cong if there was to be any chance of defeating the insurgency.

Unbeknownst to the Americans, the North Vietnamese communist party under the powerful leadership of Secretary General Le Duan had solidified its grip over the Viet Cong insurgency and committed itself to "intensifying the military struggle in order to change the balance of forces in South Vietnam and prepare for a general offensive and uprising that would lead to ultimate victory."[1] In fact, by late 1964 communist forces in the South had expanded their control over large swaths of territory and population from the central highlands to the Mekong Delta and, moreover, now operated in larger regimental-size formations that were able to not only seize rural towns, but hold them in face of government counterattacks. An upbeat Le Duan noted in early 1965 that the liberation war had "progressed by leaps and bounds," which had weakened the Saigon government to the verge of collapse and would, thus, dissuade the United States from committing troops to a land war in Asia.[2] Thus, Hanoi's all-in strategy called for an escalation of the war to reach a tipping point at a time, even as Washington still held out hope of achieving a deescalation of the fighting by threatening massive American military retaliation against the North. This put both countries squarely on a collision course.

An ongoing series of South Vietnamese government purges, military interventions, and Buddhist rioting into early 1965 complicated American efforts to formulate a coherent response.

In the meantime communist forces took advantage of the ongoing chaos, launching a series of sabotage raids on February 7 against U.S. operating bases in the central highlands that left eight Americans dead, 123 wounded, and nearly two dozen planes and helicopters destroyed or damaged.[3] Then a few days later ten Viet Cong operatives detonated explosives that leveled the Viet Cuong Hotel in Qui Nhon, which housed U.S. military personnel, leaving 23 Americans and seven Vietnamese dead and dozens injured.

The Battle For Laos: Vietnam's Proxy War 1955–1975

As part of Operation Momentum, the CIA sought to train, equip, and support a powerful force of anti-communist Hmong fighters. (Photo Hmong Archives)

Enough was enough for President Johnson. "They are killing our men while they sleep," Johnson fumed, and "we have kept our guns over the mantle ... for a long time" with little to show for our restraint.[4] Johnson ordered retaliatory air strikes by U.S. Air Force and Navy against targets in the southern panhandle of North Vietnam. While the strikes inflicted only light damage, Johnson was sending a message of his newfound willingness to up the ante. Hanoi needed to end its support to the Viet Cong and to cease its aggression in the South or face the consequences. Within a month, the first American combat troops would wade ashore at Da Nang and Operation Rolling Thunder—the first U.S. sustained air campaign against North Vietnamese territory—would be launched. Le Duan's strategy had backfired terribly, but so too the United States found itself heading down the path of ever-increasing military escalation in a conflict that it had tried so hard to avoid.

By the end of the year, Washington would have committed 184,000 troops to the fight in South Vietnam, a number that would more than double by the end of 1966 to 385,000. American ground forces would actively be engaged in counterinsurgency operations across the entire country. Likewise, the air campaign against the North would be gaining pace with Air Force and Navy pilots flying nearly 80,000 sorties and dropping more than 100,000 tons of bombs in 1966 on a variety of economic and military targets from the demilitarized zone to the outskirts of Hanoi and Haiphong.[5] In what was rapidly becoming the largest American military commitment since 1945, the escalating war on the Vietnamese peninsula would become the centerpiece of U.S. security concerns in Southeast Asia and push the ongoing conflict in Laos into the shadows.

General Vang Pao reviewing Hmong troops; he would command an army of more than 30,000 by the late 1960s. (Photo Hmong Archives)

Implications for Laos

Not only would Laos now be relegated to the backburner of U.S. concerns, but the conflict there would become nearly completely subsumed by American military strategy in Vietnam. Over the course of the next eight years, events playing out across the border in neighboring North and South Vietnam would ultimately dictate the pace, direction, and resolution of the Laotian conflict. As such it would leave the fate of the kingdom not in the hands of the Lao people, but in the hands of the Americans and Vietnamese, who were bent on advancing their own agendas in the country.

The early stages of the war in Laos consisted mainly of a series of disjointed engagements and isolated struggles for control over key towns in the northeast and along the eastern edge of the panhandle. This would begin to change by the early 1960s with the strategic focus shifting to the Plain of Jars, which takes its name from the large stone jars—some standing more than six feet tall and weighing over ten tons—that are found at various sites across the plateau and thought to be the remains of early megalithic culture. The plain was the most suitable corridor for threatening the royal capital at Luang Prabang or the government administration in Vientiane and as such it would witness some of the heaviest fighting between 1960 and 1973 as each side struggled mightily to maintain control of key towns, road junctions, and transportation routes. Major offensives were quickly met by counteroffensives with neither side able to gain a clear military advantage. Pathet Lao and North Vietnamese manpower and equipment advantages were offset by Lao and Western air support to government forces and the ability of air power to interdict the enemy's extended lines of supplies. Not surprisingly, the plain would become one of the most heavily bombed areas of Laos, leaving a legacy of unexploded ordnance that lingers to this day.

It would also become the venue for the opening round of Washington's secret war in Laos in the early 1960s. The fortuitous meeting between Vang Pao and the CIA's Bill Lair

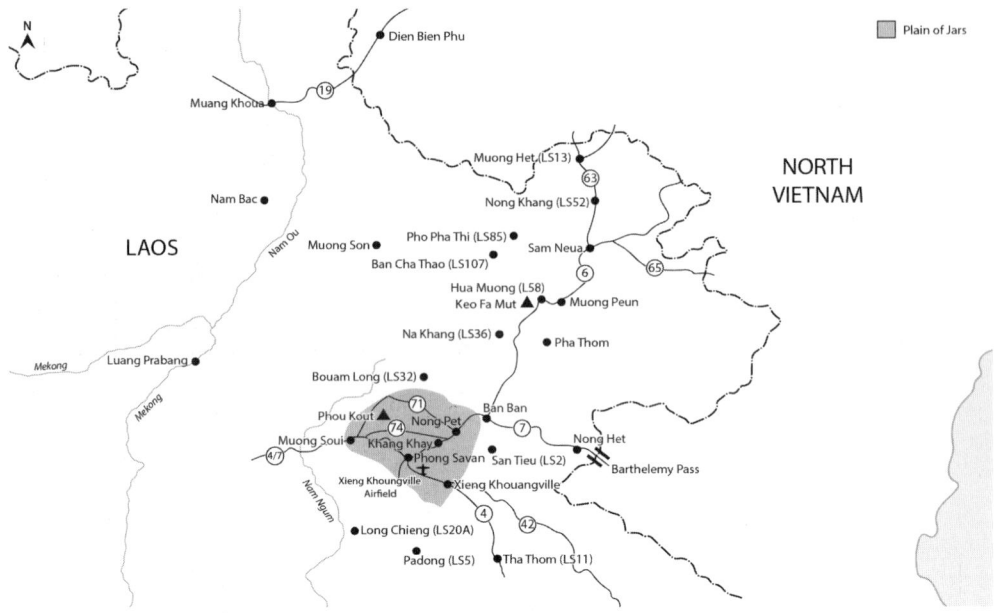

Northern Laos and the Plain of Jars.

in January 1961 at the Hmong leader's Padong base set the stage for the creation of the largest covert paramilitary effort in U.S. history. Under Operation Momentum the CIA would spend the next 12 years helping to train and equip Hmong and other Lao mountain tribesmen into an effective fighting force, "a kind of Southeast Asian maquis."[6]

The advantages of Momentum were striking. The Hmong fighters were cost effective with each soldier getting about $3 per month, easy to train using American and Lao-speaking Thai advisers, and cheap to arm with light weapons. They were also likely to be more effective than the unwieldy and hard-to-control national army, because they would operate with CIA direction from mountain bases in guerrilla fashion to attack and then fade back into the countryside.[7] Moreover, they would have the full backing of the CIA's Air America logistics capability, as well as the ability to coordinate U.S. air support operations through CIA officers in the field. In time, the effort surpassed everyone's wildest dreams with General Vang Pao eventually commanding an almost 40,000-strong force that became a deep thorn in the side of the Pathet Lao and North Vietnamese.

Through the use of massive U.S. military assistance to the Souvanna government, the development of the CIA's secret Hmong army, and extensive military cooperation and coordination with Thailand, the United States became largely successful in stymieing communist attempts to gain greater control over Lao territory. Most important of all, this approach enabled Washington to continue to adhere to the fiction of a "neutral Laos" by finding creative ways to circumvent the second Geneva conference agreement of 1962, which admittedly the North Vietnamese had been violating since the beginning of the agreement. Nonetheless, the myth of a demilitarized Laos would continue to be preserved despite the country's ever-growing entanglement in the Vietnam War.

While the contest over the Plain of Jars would still continue to occupy the attention of the warring Lao factions, America's rising commitment in Vietnam would dictate a marked shift of emphasis to southern Laos. For now the primary threat emanating from the country was that of North Vietnamese infiltration of men and matériel into the South via the Ho Chi Minh Trail. If the Saigon government and the Americans were to have any chance of military victory, this flow would need to be severely curtailed. In return for granting Washington near carte blanche to conduct an air interdiction campaign in the panhandle, the United States would quietly continue to assist the Souvanna government in its fight against the Pathet Lao and their North Vietnamese allies. It would be a marriage of convenience that had benefits for all.

CIA paramilitary officers played a prominent role in the field by advising and helping direct combat operations.

Despite the fundamental nature of American involvement in Laos remaining relatively the same, the scope and intensity of U.S. involvement—especially with regard to the air war being waged over the country—would witness a number of dramatic changes in the coming years. Although Air America transports and Thai-piloted T-28 aircraft had played an important role in providing RLAF support to embattled FAR and Neutralist forces, the start of Operation Barrel Roll in December 1964 marked a milestone in American military assistance. For the first time, U.S. Air Force and Navy strike aircraft would be directly targeting Pathet Lao and North Vietnamese lines of supply and communication in northern and central Laos in a sustained aerial interdiction effort. Likewise, in April 1965 the U.S. Air Force conducted its first interdiction missions against North Vietnamese troop and supply movements in the panhandle of Laos, signaling the start of Operation Steel Tiger. By the time both air campaigns ended nearly eight years later, Laos would have become one of the most heavily bombed countries in the world.

William Sullivan's War

The most unusual and striking aspect of the American war effort in Laos, however, was its decidedly "civilian flavor." For unlike in Vietnam where the U.S. military was squarely in charge of operational decisions and the deployment of men and equipment through a multilayered chain of command, the U.S. ambassador to Laos ran the entire show. This stemmed from two key presidential policy decisions made in the early 1960s

Left: The CIA made extensive use of leaflet drops over Pathet Lao territory to stoke anti-communist sentiment. (Photo Museum of the U.S. Air Force)

Below: The Thai air base at Udorn served an important role in supporting Lao T-28 pilot training under Project Water Pump that began in early 1964. (Photo Museum of the U.S. Air Force)

by President Kennedy. First, in an effort to empower and improve the effectiveness of the State Department Kennedy sent a letter to each U.S. ambassador underscoring their position as the president's sole representative in-country and their complete authority over all U.S. operations and agencies, except American military forces operating in the field under the command of a U.S. area commander.[8] Thus, by default, where the United States was engaged in military activities, e.g. Laos after the October 1962 Geneva agreements, without an area military commander the ambassador's authority was supreme. Second, the Kennedy administration policy of "neutralizing Laos" effectively transferred the Laotian problem "from the military arena to the political arena."[9] As such, the U.S. ambassador to Laos presided over nearly every aspect of American military engagement in the Laotian war, drawing a stark contrast between the conflicts in Laos and Vietnam from the very beginning.

The CIA's Man in Laos: General Vang Pao

For some fifteen years prior to his exile to the United States in 1975, the Hmong leader, General Vang Pao, served as the commander of the CIA's covert guerrilla army battling Pathet Lao and North Vietnamese forces in Laos and was called by former CIA Director William Colby—who served as chief of the CIA's Southeast Asia Division during the war—as "the biggest hero of the Vietnam War."

A man of slight physical stature, Vang Pao nonetheless commanded great respect among his fellow Hmong tribesmen for his devotion to his people, sharp mind, and manic energy. "He was an extremely good leader [and] worshiped by his troops," according to a former CIA officer. An ardent anti-communist, who worked his way up the ranks of the French colonial and Laotian armies to become commanding general of the central military region of Laos in 1964, a 31-year-old Vang Pao was tapped by the CIA in early 1961 to build a force of several thousand guerrilla fighters to stem the communist advance across Laos. Operation Momentum was born.

Funded, trained, and equipped by the CIA, along with assistance from Thai paramilitary troops, the so-called "secret army" grew to nearly 40,000 men and soon became the cornerstone of government military operations in central Laos. From 1969 to 1971 Vang Pao directed numerous large-scale offensives on the Plain of Jars, where his Hmong fighters slugged it out with Pathet Lao and North Vietnamese troops, scoring several major victories in the process. However, by 1972 his forces were spent and exhausted from years of fighting and heavy casualties. The final blow for Vang Pao came with the signing of the 1973 Paris peace agreement that brought an end to U.S. military involvement in Southeast Asia. It also brought an end to American support to the Hmong.

Not surprisingly, a shaky ceasefire in Laos failed to keep the peace. Without American support, the remaining anti-communist resistance crumbled and the Pathet Lao came to power in May 1975, bringing an end to the civil war. Vang Pao and several thousand of his men and their families were airlifted to Thailand, but the majority of Hmong fighters forced to fend for themselves. Fearing harsh communist reprisals tens of thousands fled to safety across the Mekong River into Thailand and became refugees. Other Hmong decided to stay and continue the fight against the new communist government for the next decade.

(Sources: M. Stuart-Fox and M. Kooyman, *Historical Dictionary of Laos*; *Christian Science Monitor*, "The Life of General Vang Pao, Hmong Guerrilla Leader.")

The Battle For Laos: Vietnam's Proxy War 1955–1975

Above: U.S. Marines come ashore at Da Nang, South Vietnam, in March 1965 signaling the start of America's direct military involvement in the war. (Photo Museum of the U.S. Air Force)

Below: Within a year of their arrival American troops would be heavily engaged in South Vietnamese combat operations as the war intensified.

Hanoi's development of Laotian panhandle as a conduit for supporting the war in South Vietnam made Laos's entanglement in that conflict all but inevitable.

From November 1964 to March 1969, Ambassador William H. Sullivan served in this role, overseeing America's secret war in Laos "in such a way as to preserve the façade of American adherence to the Geneva agreements."[10] Widely considered a talented diplomat with solid credentials (he served as Harriman's deputy during the Geneva talks on Laos), Sullivan wielded his authority and clout with an iron fist—requiring all U.S. government activities in Laos, some Lao military operations, and all American air and ground operations within the country's border to have his prior approval.[11] With the Johnson administration's focus on fighting the war in Vietnam and not addressing the political challenge in Laos, Sullivan's authority remained largely unquestioned. This of course, did not prevent U.S. commanders in Southeast Asia from chaffing at Sullivan's role and involvement "in purely military matters," especially with respect to the Laotian southern panhandle.[12]

While this pragmatic division of labor certainly served to maintain the fig leaf of American neutrality during the entire Laotian civil war, head off any unwanted direct Soviet or Chinese intervention in the conflict, and avoided having Washington commit U.S. ground troops in Laos, it almost certainly too hamstrung American military efforts to turn the tide of battle in both Laos and South Vietnam during the latter half of the 1960s.

Sullivan's strong distrust of the military led him to exclude Military Assistance Command Vietnam (MACV) and Air Force commanders from his decision-making process and complicated efforts by U.S. military advisers (now based in Thailand following the Geneva Agreements) to supervise and gauge the effectiveness of American training and assistance efforts. Under Sullivan's tenure, no targets in the country were attacked

The Battle For Laos: Vietnam's Proxy War 1955–1975

Above left: U.S. Ambassador William Sullivan exercised firm control over America's secret war in Laos, something that dismayed U.S. military commanders.

Above right: President Lyndon Johnson meeting with Prime Minister Souvanna at the White House in October 1967. (Photo LBJ Presidential Library)

without his permission and he held sway over detailed operational decisions, such as which outpost to evacuate, reinforce or support with air strikes.[13] All this was done without the need to consult any American military officials. This effort to keep the U.S. military at arm's length for what were seen as valid foreign policy reasons, however, elevated the military role of the CIA to new heights. And for much of the decade the Agency became the main conduit for projecting military power within Laos. The civilians were clearly in control of the American war effort.

The consequences of this arrangement on the battlefield were telling. The war was handled in a very ad hoc manner with little long-term strategic planning or well-defined military strategy. Lacking little accountability and U.S. military supervision, the FAR continued its subpar performance in combat despite the large amount of American military equipment flowing into the country. While Vang Pao's Hmong irregulars had become the tip of the American spear in Laos by the mid-1960s thanks to CIA efforts, the Agency's desire to employ these fighters in a more conventional role against battle-tested North Vietnamese troops was misguided. CIA officers were also ill-suited to take full advantage of American military air power and were often criticized for their poor or ineffective use of U.S. Air Force assets based in Thailand. Fortunately, the Pathet Lao's often weak combat performance and Hanoi's central focus on keeping open its lines of supply and communication through southern Laos prevented communist forces from exploiting these weaknesses during Sullivan's tenure.

This legacy of treating Laos early on as primarily a political problem that required complete civilian control and warranted only limited U.S. military engagement helped sow the seeds of eventual failure, not only in Laos but also in neighboring South Vietnam

Into the Vietnamese Quagmire

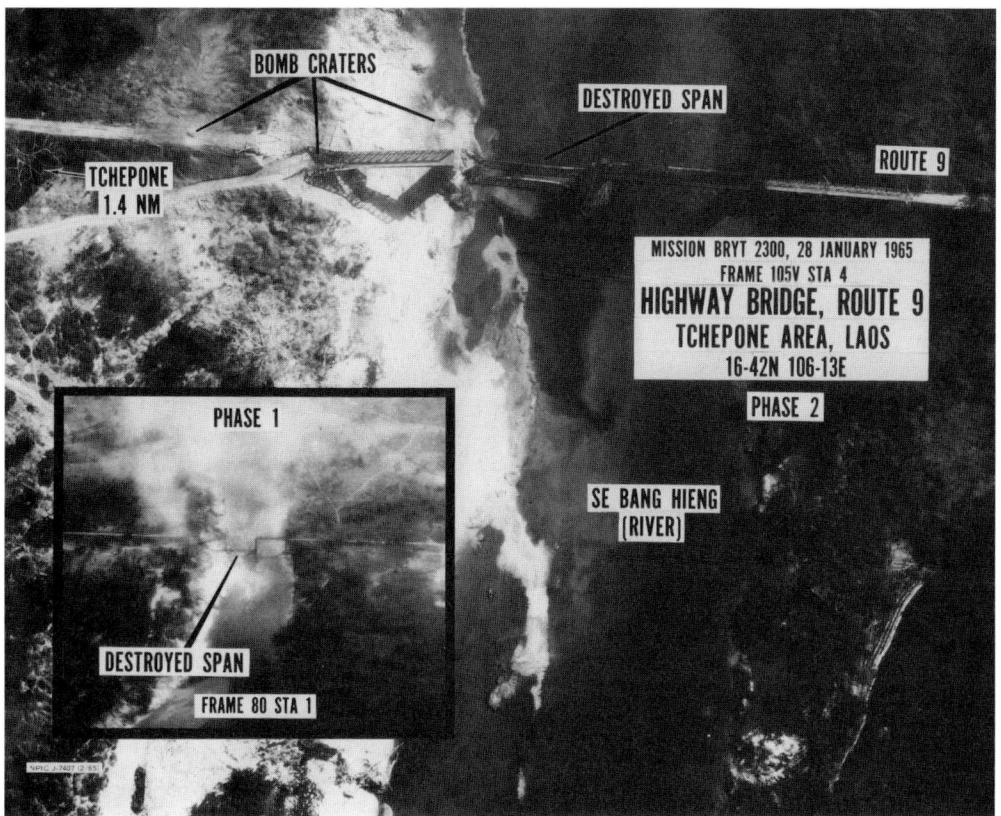

Bomb damage assessment of an air attack on a highway bridge over the Bang Hieng River near Tchepone in southern Laos, January 1965. (Photo Museum of the U.S. Air Force)

in the 1970s. Although the conflicts in each country followed their own unique path, both would become increasingly linked as the growing American military commitment to South Vietnam forced the hands of its neighbors. By the mid-1960s a wider regional war was in the offing that all parties would find impossible to avoid.

4. RAISING THE STAKES

Now with America's direct military intervention in the Vietnam, the war in Laos entered a new stage that would reshape the future course of war. Laos would now be completely entangled in the Vietnamese conflict—a fate it and U.S. policymakers had tried so hard to avoid—with events on the Vietnamese peninsula profoundly influencing the ebb and flow of the fighting. Moreover, success or failure for the Americans in Vietnam would all but certainly determine success or failure in neighboring Laos. The stakes were now higher than ever before.

Not surprisingly, political events dominated the beginning of this period when General Phoumi launched yet another coup in late January 1965. The attempted military putsch failed and General Kouprasith Abhay, the commander of the Vientiane military region, used the opportunity to crush Phoumi and his ally General Siho. Both men were then forced into exile in Thailand. The resulting division of spoils and consolidation of power among Kouprasith's fellow rightist generals saw a further decentralization of command with each of the five military regional commanders becoming a de facto warlord and acting in their own personal and financial interest. Naturally this complicated the prosecution of war, as well as Washington's ongoing efforts to restructure the FAR into an effective counterinsurgency force. The burden of fighting would now increasingly fall on Vang Pao's Hmong army and the growing use of, and dependence on, American air power to stem the communist advance. Laos was also being transformed into two distinctly different battlegrounds. One venue in the center and northeast pitted government forces with CIA assistance against the Pathet Lao and their North Vietnamese allies. The other being fought in the south of the country pitted American air power against the North Vietnamese logistics network feeding the escalating war in South Vietnam. While the outcome on either battlefront was far from being decided at this point, it was all but certain the intensity of these struggles would rise to new heights in the years ahead.

The Northern Battlefield's Opening Round

As part of their dry-season offensive in northern Laos, communist forces in early 1965 moved to strengthen their control over western portions of Sam Neua Province by securing lines of supply and communication along Route 6 that connected the provincial capital to the Plain of Jars. This meant clearing out Vang Pao's guerrillas from their mountaintop enclaves in the area. Their main target was the large Hmong encampment at Hua Muong and Lima Site 58 (LS 58) on the Sang Ca River, some 30 miles southwest of Sam Neua city.

On January 20 the Hmong base at Ban Hong Non fell to attacking Pathet Lao and North Vietnamese troops, as did other smaller outposts north and east of Hua Muong, as the clearing operation gained pace. Adding to the threat, enemy forces to south also began

U.S. Air Force F-105 Thunderchiefs would play a major role in supporting Lao government forces as part of Barrel Roll operations over northern Laos. (Photo U.S. Air Force)

advancing northward from Ban Ban at the end of the month, overrunning Muong Khao and Pha Tom in early February. With the vice closing around Hua Muong by some 1,500 enemy troops, Vang Pao ordered the evacuation of the women, the elderly, and children. Over the course of two days Air America C-7 Caribou transports flying into LS 58 airlifted several thousand to safety. Unfortunately, this humanitarian gesture precipitated a breakdown in discipline as Hmong soldiers abandoned their posts to join their now-departed families; Hua Muong fell with little resistance on February 14.[1]

Falling back to Na Khang and LS 36, the final line of Hmong resistance in the province, Ambassador Sullivan and U.S. advisers began to fear the worst as efforts to cajole Kong Le into aiding the defense found the general at Muong Soui too busy haggling with his battalion commanders over finances, promotions, and blame over poor battlefield performances to be bothered.[2] To slow down the advance, the U.S. Embassy urged increased RLAF strikes, as well as stepped-up Barrel Roll missions against routes 6 and 7.

Implementing new aggressive Barrel Roll missions, however, proved problematic given the myriad of rules of engagement restrictions, cumbersome Embassy–military coordination challenges, and timeliness of the strikes. For instance, a February 19 mission by eight Air Force F-105s of the 12th Tactical Fighter Squadron (TFS) out of Da Nang to attack a large truck convoy and artillery battery 20 miles southwest of Sam Neua city instead ended up hitting trucks and buildings on the outskirts of the city when the F-105s came across them as targets of opportunity. The original target thus escaped unscathed, much to the unhappiness of Ambassador Sullivan and the Lao government.[3]

Over the course of the next several weeks efforts were made to streamline the process, but the initiation, approval, and tasking process that ran through Vientiane, MACV in Saigon, Washington, and back to MACV still remained unwieldy. More effective, however, was Sullivan's desire to base reactive strike aircraft in Thailand rather than in South Vietnam or on U.S. aircraft carriers in the Gulf of Tonkin. By May two F-4 Phantoms at Ubon

The Battle For Laos: Vietnam's Proxy War 1955–1975

The unassuming, yet strategically located, Hmong base at Na Khang and Lima Site 36 would become the scene of vicious battles between 1966 and 1968. (Photo Museum of the U.S. Air Force)

and two F-105 Thunderchiefs at Korat were being placed on alert for rapid response and were in addition to preprogramed Barrel Roll missions. This action paid dividends almost immediately when a flight of Phantoms was called in to assist Lao T-28s attacking a group of North Vietnamese tanks operating just north of the Plain of Jars near Muong Kheung on May 9. Four tanks were reported destroyed and seven more damaged in the air strikes.[4]

By mid-year the communist offensive in the northeast had ground to a halt with the approach of the monsoon rains and short of capturing Na Khang. Their overextended and now regularly bombed supply lines also forced the enemy to consolidate his gains and await an expected government counteroffensive. They would not have to wait long.

From his new forward command post at Na Khang and LS 36, Vang Pao was busy making plans to recapture positions lost earlier in the year. His first order of business would be to neutralize the enemy position on Keo Fa Mut, a 6,000-foot-high mountain on a ridge line that blocked his line of advance on Hua Muong. Encountering stiff resistance by the well-entrenched defenders, Vang Pao called in air strikes on July 21. More than 40 Lao T-28 sorties were flown using white phosphorus munitions, while American jets pounded the mountaintop with 750-pound high-explosive bombs.[5] On the ground Air Force and CIA air liaison teams helped direct the relentless air attack, which allowed Vang Pao to capture the position without any further resistance on July 28. Government casualties were light, while upwards of 200 communist troops were killed in the battle.

After regrouping and mopping up any remaining resistance in the area, Vang Pao pushed northeast toward Hua Muong by mid-August. Bad weather hindered air support at first, but the skies cleared enough in mid-September to allow strafing runs by T-28s to soften up the defenses surrounding Hua Muong. In the meantime, American jets repeatedly struck the eastern end of Route 6 to prevent reinforcements from arriving and on September 21 Vang Pao's troops reentered the city.

During the course of the two-month campaign, the RLAF had flown nearly 800 sorties and the American almost another 300 that relentlessly attacked the enemy. Air power had clearly made a telling difference. It allowed Vang Pao's forces to blast the enemy from well-defended positions at minimal cost to attacking ground troops and significantly hindered enemy resupply efforts. Ambassador Sullivan believed that not only had air power broken the back of the enemy, but it helped put an "aggressive drive into friendly forces."[6]

Air Power to the Rescue

The ground war in the north now took on what would become a familiar seasonal pattern, with communist forces advancing during the dry season from November to March with their tanks and artillery only to fall back on their overextended and bogged-down supply lines during the rainy season from April to October in the face of government counteroffensives. Although skirmishing and Barrel Roll air strikes continued across the Plain of Jars throughout 1966, the bulk of the fighting would take place on the western edge of the plain near the main Neutralist base at Muong Soui and in Military Regions I and II north of the plain.

Frustrated by past failures to retake Phou Kout Mountain overlooking Route 7 that was about ten miles east of his base at Muong Soui, Kong Le proposed to neutralize the position with massive American air strikes. This would then allow his men to bypass the position and establish a firm bridgehead on the Plain of Jars. Unfortunately, on February 1, 1966 President Johnson ended a 37-day bombing halt over North Vietnam (intended to cajole Hanoi into negotiations) and the anticipated U.S. aircraft were not available. The burden of air support then fell on the overstretched RLAF and soon the feeble ground attack sputtered and died.

About the same time some 80 miles to the northeast, communist troops resumed their efforts to gain control over Route 6. They overran the government position at Houei Thom on February 12 and then set their

The Air America compound at Udorn, Thailand, served as a hub of operations. (Photo Museum of the U.S. Air Force)

sights on Vang Pao's base at Na Khang. Over the course of three days in mid-February the defenders of Na Khang once again found themselves facing a determined enemy assault. Three mass assaults on the airstrip and support compound were repulsed thanks to stiff resistance by the Hmong fighters and heavy U.S. air support called in by orbiting American FACs—a free-spirited group of former Air Force and Army forward air controllers under contract to the U.S. Embassy that would become known by their call sign as the Ravens. The increasingly desperate battle also saw the first use in Laos of an AC-47 gunship firing 6,000 rounds per minute, as well as the first use of napalm.[7] The enemy, however, kept coming and by the evening of February 19 the last Hmong fighter was airlifted from the base. A flight of F-105s then rolled in, destroying any abandoned equipment and supplies, as well as scores of occupying soldiers with a devastating napalm strike. Refugee accounts later reported seeing dead North Vietnamese soldiers "strewn about like tree stumps, estimating more than one thousand casualties." Taking Na Khang had come at a steep price for the enemy.

The battle was also noteworthy for coming within a hair's breadth of changing the future course of the war. Shortly after his arrival on the morning of February 18 to take personal command, Vang Pao was wounded by an errant bullet that struck him in the right arm and chest. He was immediately evacuated by an Air America H-34 helicopter to Korat, Thailand, for urgent medical treatment.[8] (He would also later undergo reconstructive surgery for his arm at Tripler Army Medical Center in Honolulu, Hawaii.) While recovering in Thailand, the Pathet Lao began to announce the death of Vang Pao, which caused a "pall to fall over the Hmong upon hearing the news."[9] The general responded by making a tape recording and reassuring his people that he was still alive and well. Had Vang Pao been killed at Na Khang, however, it is entirely likely that the Hmong army would have fragmented and with it the primary line of defense against an early communist victory in Laos by the late 1960s.

While potential disaster had been averted, the loss of Na Khang, Houei Thom, and then Muong Heim in early March 1966 left the Souvanna government in a precarious state. Not only had the communists secured their supply lines down Route 6, but now Kong Le's position at Muong Soui was completely exposed. The garrison was the last remaining government outpost on the western edge of the Plain of Jars and its fall would open the door to the vital Route 13 corridor connecting Vientiane and Luang Prabang.

To relieve the mounting pressure, Neutralist troops launched yet another attempt to seize the high ground of Phou Kout on March 14. Following a massive air bombardment that included the use of napalm by American jets, Kong Le's troops scrambled to the top of the mountain. Unfortunately, they found themselves caught in a deadly crossfire from bunker complexes on the surrounding hills. A failed attempt to roust the North Vietnamese defenders from these positions failed and by March 20 elements of two Pathet Lao battalions counterattacked and swept the Neutralists from the mountain.

Despite suffering only light casualties in the battle and still outnumbering the communist forces encircling Muong Soui, Ambassador Sullivan was increasingly concerned that the Kong Le's men would "simply fold up and run" and the FAR generals showed no inclination to assist their shaky ally.[10] To encourage the defenders to "pull up their socks

The Thai Factor

Throughout the entire period of U.S. military engagement in Southeast Asia, Thailand remained steadfast as one of Washington's most essential—yet behind the scenes—Cold War allies in the regional struggle to stem communist expansion. From the granting of basing and operating rights for hundreds of aircraft and thousands of U.S. military personnel on Thai soil to the provision of large numbers of military "volunteers" and its extensive intelligence and diplomacy cooperation with the United States, Bangkok's role was critical. Nowhere was this truer than with respect to the secret war in Laos, where Thai support became indispensable to American covert operations and the survival of the anti-communist forces.

The central component of America's secret war in Laos, the creation of General Vang Pao's Hmong army, could not have been successfully accomplished without the extensive training assistance and operational participation of dozens of Thai paramilitary advisers. Some were individually recruited by the CIA from the Lao-speaking parts of northeast Thailand, but the majority were Police Aerial Reinforcement Unit (PARU) personnel, the Thai quick-reaction force developed by the CIA's Bill Lair in the early 1950s. Over time the PARU advisers would be replaced by Thai army personnel seconded to the Lao military and by a growing number of CIA paramilitary officers. In March 1970, regular Thai army units—many paid for and equipped by the CIA—were secretly deployed to Laos and would soon comprise about 25 percent of Vang Pao's forces before they were eventually withdrawn from Laos in June 1974.

Even prior to this surge, hundreds of Thai volunteers had been dispatched to Laos to shore up government forces at critical times early on in the war. Thai-contracted T-28 pilots flew alongside their Royal Lao Air Force counterparts to provide badly needed close air support, providing about half the needed sorties in the mid-1960s. Likewise, volunteer Thai artillery units equipped with American-made 105-mm and 155-mm howitzers served as desperately needed stiffeners for FAR and Neutralist troops during the battles on the western Plain of Jars in 1968/9.

Just as important as its commitment of manpower, was Bangkok's provision of secure rear operating bases and facilities in Thailand for the CIA, the U.S military, and for training Lao military personnel. From Air America's primary operating base at Udorn to the special operations squadrons at Nakhon Phanom on the Mekong River and the other five major Air Force bases in Thailand, the United States was able to sustain air operations over Laos that undoubtedly helped ensure the survival of the Vientiane government. Other covert facilities in the country, such as the CIA's 4802nd Joint Liaison Detachment, worked closely with the Thai military to coordinate intelligence collection activities in Laos; still others functioned as advanced training centers for Lao military personnel.

(Sources: M. Stuart-Fox and M. Kooyman, *Historical Dictionary of Laos*, pp. 152-3; T. Castle, *At War in the Shadow of Vietnam*, pp. 60-1)

Civilian Air America pilots standing in front of an Air America PC-6 Porter utility aircraft.

and make a determined stand," Sullivan requested the Seventh Air Force out of Thailand immediately launch a series of intense air strikes around Muong Soui, as well as against key targets on the plain. In response Thunderchiefs pounded the Ban Liang military complex near Khang Khay, destroying over 25 buildings and flew nearly 200 close air support sorties in the Muong Soui area.[11]

Still the situation remained precarious with the FAR General Staff lamenting the poor performance of the Neutralists and wondering why so many American aircraft were being used in the Laotian panhandle when the real battle was being fought for control over the Plain of Jars. Sullivan's reassurances to the Lao generals aside, he and MACV commander General William Westmoreland remained at odds over the importance of the war in northern Laos to the Southeast Asian theater. Eventually Westmoreland acknowledged the political—if not the military—necessity of supporting Sullivan's requests for more Barrel Roll sorties as a de facto quid for increased support for Steel Tiger operations.[12] Ultimately, the U.S. air response and the onset of the rainy season put an end to the immediate threat to Muong Soui as communist forces pulled back in anticipation of a government rainy season offensive.

Going on the Offensive

They would not have to wait long for Vang Pao to act. Muong Heim was retaken on May 10 and by May 23 the communist troops at Na Khang were nearly surrounded. Fortuitously, bad weather over North Vietnam diverted an 18-plane Rolling Thunder strike to support the attack on Na Khang on May 23. The Air Force jets swept in to release 54,000 pounds of high explosives on the unsuspecting defenders, killing at least 300 of the enemy.[13] The base fell shortly thereafter; Na Khang and LS 36 were back in government hands. By June, Vang Pao's forces were able to reestablish themselves along Route 6 and threaten the communist flow of supplies southward to the Plain of Jars. Other guerrilla units pushed even farther north that summer, extending their operations virtually up to the North Vietnamese border.

Meanwhile, the FAR with the support of Vang Pao's troops and the RLAF finally returned to the offensive in mid-July. The objective of Operation Prasane was to clear Pathet Lao forces from Nam Bac and the Ou river valley in northeastern Luang Prabang Province. If successful, the government would achieve a major psychological victory and, moreover, be able to block the traditional invasion route from Dien Bein Phu southwestward to the royal capital at Luang Prabang. The operation got underway on July 18 with T-28s out of Luang Prabang softening up targets and landing sites. Some additional 1,400 troops were then airlifted by Air America aircraft into position to join other ground troops enveloping Nam Bac. The town fell to government troops after a brief fight on August 7.

Even as the war ground on in the north of the country, long simmering personal rivalries and political intrigue by senior commanders in the FAR General Staff triggered a major crisis in mid-October. Generals Ouane and Kouprasith had long wanted to bring the roughly 12,000-man Neutralist army under their direct control and Kong Le's ineffectiveness during the Phou Kout campaign encouraged them to provoke dissention within the Neutralist ranks. Spurred by offers of promotions in a newly reorganized FAR, Kong Le's once loyal lieutenants turned on him. The general was ousted in a bloodless coup on October 16 and Kong Le flew into exile in Thailand the next day.

At the same time a bitter and increasingly personal feud between General Kouprasith and General Thao Ma, the RLAF commander, came to head. Kouprasith wanted to get rid of Thao Ma, because he believed the air force commander was too independent-minded and overly responsive to American needs. Moreover, Thao Ma had made enemies within the General Staff by refusing to carry out orders he suspected were for personal gain, which included the use of RLAF C-47s to transport opium and smuggle gold. Believing his days were numbered, Thao Ma made a last-ditch effort to take down his enemies by launching an air attack on the FAR headquarters in Vientiane on the morning of October 21. Thao Ma, however, failed to provoke any wider rebellion. Finding himself alone and isolated and fearing the worst, he and 25 of his pilots flew their T-28s across the border to Udorn the next day and requested political asylum from the Thai government.

While the bulk of the RLAF was disappearing into exile, efforts were underway by the Americans to improve cooperation and coordination between the U.S. Embassy Vientiane and the Seventh Air Force in Thailand, now under the command of General William Momyer. Revised procedures, updated protocols, and discussions over sorties allocations for Barrel Roll and Steel Tiger resulted in Momyer's commitment to flying nearly three dozen sorties per day in northern Laos. These sorties would include for the first time the A-26K Counter Invader. The A-26K was an update version of the old B-26 bomber that was heavily armed with up to 14 fixed .50-caliber machine guns and the capability to carry 4,000 pounds of armaments on eight external pylons.[14] Attached to the 606th Air Commando Squadron (ACS) at Nakhon Phanom, Thailand, these aircraft would be used to counter the expected increase in enemy nighttime truck traffic during the dry-season campaign buildup. Working in conjunction with CIA road-watch teams during nighttime missions in early November, the A-26s scored multiple successes by destroying more than

The venerable A-1 Skyraider with its large payloads and endurance would quickly become the mainstay of American close air support to General Vang Pao's army by the mid-1960s. (Photo Museum of the U.S. Air Force)

60 trucks and killing at least 300 enemy soldiers.[15] Bad weather for the remainder of the month, however, greatly hindered U.S. interdiction efforts and the Pathet Lao and North Vietnamese were able to continue their stockpiling of supplies.

As 1966 drew toward a close, government forces had made some headway in rolling back communist forces in the northeast, but these gains remained precarious. Overall, the situation on the Plain of Jars remained largely unchanged with communist forces holding the bulk of the territory, while the now-combined FAR–Neutralist force at Muong Soui clung to its toehold on the western edge. To the south of the plain in Xieng Khouang Province, the dividing line roughly along Route 4 also remained relatively static as well. Government forces had a slight numerical advantage—although quality varied greatly—in military manpower with U.S. intelligence estimating the size of the communist forces in Laos at approximately 40,000 men. This number included some 7,500 North Vietnamese infantry and another 5,000 advisers attached to Pathet Lao units, but did not include the roughly 30,000 North Vietnamese troops attached to Group 559 in the panhandle supporting Ho Chi Minh Trail operations.[16]

The Northern Battlefield: Round Two

The communist 1966/7 dry-season offensive kicked off in late November with an attack by Pathet Lao forces on Tha Thom, about 35 miles southeast of Khang Khay. The town changed hands several times before finally being recaptured by FAR reinforcements flown into the battle. Casualties were light on both sides, but the Pathet Lao troops were able to seize a large supply of ammunition before retreating. Meanwhile, the anticipated seasonal attack on Muong Soui failed to materialize. The reason soon became apparent. Once again the main communist thrust would be aimed at clearing government troops away from their Route 6 supply lines, as well as eliminating the government salient at Nam Bac in the northeast.

Not unexpectedly, Vang Pao's base at Na Khang was the first target. On the night of January 5, 1967 North Vietnamese sappers began to infiltrate the position, but were discovered and a firefight ensued. At dawn two battalions from the North Vietnamese

General Vang Pao calls in American close air support against attacking communist forces.

Army's (NVA) 174th Regiment launched a series of wave attacks against the 500 Hmong defenders. Taking advantage of the solid overcast that hindered any potential air support, the soldiers pushed the defenders steadily back toward their main compound and last line of defense. Eight arriving Air Force F-105s tried in vain to find a break in the dense cloud cover, but were stymied.

It was only the timely arrival of two A-1 Skyraiders from the 602nd Fighter Commando Squadron out of Udorn that saved the day. Diving down through the dangerous overcast, first one and then the other Skyraider blasted the attacking NVA troops with 20-mm cannon fire, 100-pound white-phosphorus bombs, and 2.75-inch rockets. They bought enough time for the weather to clear and have a Raven FAC direct overlapping flights of F-104s, F-105s, A-1s, and T-28s against the remaining enemy. By the next day the North Vietnamese had had enough and broke off the attack, leaving at least 63 dead on the battlefield and carrying away scores more dead and wounded.[17]

Shifting their attention to safeguarding the western segment of Route 6 running through Sam Neua Province, communist forces then launched an assault on Nong Khang, some 15 miles north of Sam Neua city. North Vietnamese infantry swept forward following a mortar barrage in the early hours of January 22. Quickly the battle devolved into bitter hand-to-hand fighting. The timely arrival of Lao T-28s and American A-1s, however, helped turn the tide and once again the enemy was repulsed with heavy losses thanks to air power.

Seeking to even the score on the night of February 2, a 30-man North Vietnamese sapper unit sprang a surprise raid on Luang Prabang airfield. Using 40-mm rockets and automatic weapons they destroyed six Lao T-28s, damaged three more, and put three Air America H-34 helicopters out of action.[18] Five government soldiers were also killed and 75 percent of the air operations center was destroyed. Beyond the aircraft losses and damage,

The Battle For Laos: Vietnam's Proxy War 1955–1975

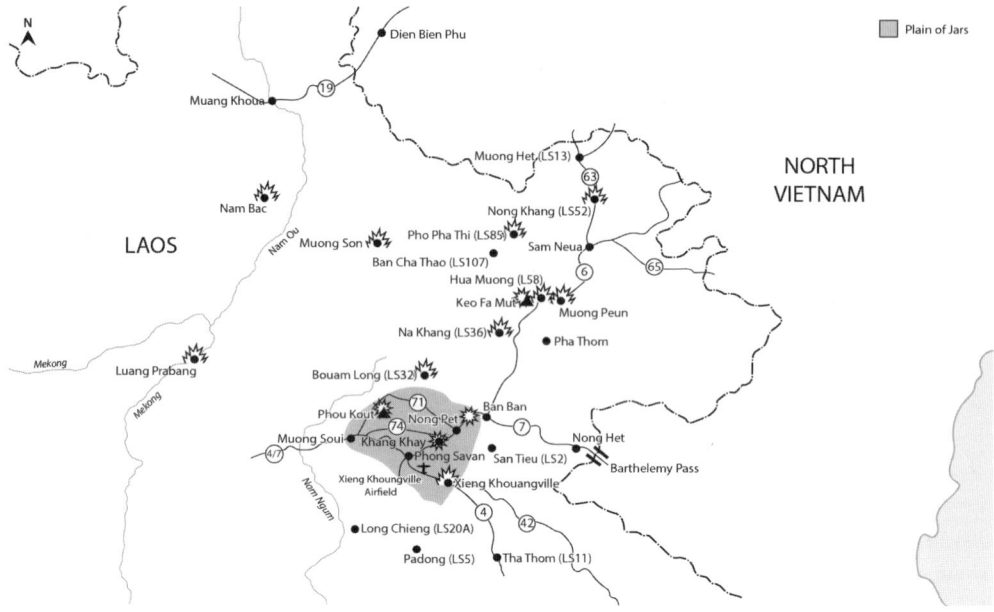

Northern Battlefield.

the raid was noteworthy for being the first communist attack on the royal capital, which heretofore had been off limits.

Aware of a government buildup at Nam Bac in preparation for its own northern offensive, communist forces in the area launched a preemptive attack on Mobile Group 11 north of the airstrip on the night of March 10. Despite some initial enemy gains, the defenders stiffened with the aid of more than 200 air strikes. With their base now secure, some 1,500 FAR and Hmong troops equipped with 105-mm howitzers advanced westward on March 12 to cut off infiltration routes and seize Ban Mok Plai as a springboard for a future attack on Muong Sai and thus secure northeast Luang Prabang Province. Ban Mok Plai fell to government forces in mid-March after a brief fight.

Over the next week, however, the retreating Ban Mok Plai troops regrouped and were soon reinforced by two NVA battalions. On March 20 this force launched an all-out assault on Ban Mok Plai. Despite extensive close air support by the RLAF, the tide began to turn against the defenders as the attack gained momentum. Several units then panicked and any semblance of a defense collapsed as soldiers fled for their lives toward Nam Bac, abandoning large amounts of equipment and supplies in the process. Any thought of retaking Muong Sai now had to be abandoned. To make matters worse, another assault on Nong Khang in early April proved successful this time when the defenders ran low on ammunition and poor weather prevented aerial resupply and close air support. The position was abandoned on April 4.

In the meantime some 35 miles to the southwest, Vang Pao had been struggling since mid-March to capture Chik Mok Lok, a 4,000-foot mountain overlooking the town of Muong Peun and the Route 6 supply lines. Repeated attempts—even with the aid of close air support—had failed to dislodge the well-entrenched defenders. Never one to give up easily, the Hmong troops were able to claw their way to the summit on April 9 as A-1s and F-105s blasted the defenders with napalm and anti-personnel bomblets. Their victory was short-lived, however, as the wounding of the Hmong commander and a fierce North Vietnamese counterattack drove the guerrillas from the mountaintop.

It wasn't all bad news for government forces. They still held on to Nam Bac, Na Khang, and several other key forward positions in the northeast. Moreover, an apparent late-March spike in vehicular traffic moving along Route 7 toward Muong Soui failed to presage another major enemy attack there. Thus, the communist dry offensive came to an end with a whimper by the end of April with the battlefield situation largely unchanged.

The 1967 rainy season in Laos came unusually late with the rains only beginning in earnest in July, but Ambassador Sullivan was upbeat about the situation and feeling that it was now time to seize the initiative.[19] There was reason for Sullivan's optimism. Government forces now outnumbered the enemy and were better trained and equipped than before and, more important, they had come through the dry season without suffering any serious defeats. The capabilities of the RLAF had been rebuilt following the ouster of Thao Ma (although it new leadership was plagued with problems) and it had demonstrated its effectiveness during the recent campaign. Likewise, the expansion of the Seventh Air Force boded well for a permanent increase in the number of Barrel Roll sorties. Recent elections had finally brought about a degree of political stability under Prime Minister Souvanna. All in all, things appeared to be looking up.

Grand Plans, but the Enemy Has a Vote

The FAR General Staff must have been feeling its oats too in planning its upcoming offensive. General Ouane's new campaign called for a widening of the Nam Bac salient by capturing Muong Sai with follow-on operations to cut the main communist supply lines—Route 19 from Dien Bien Phu, Route 6 from Sam Neua, and Route 7 from Barthelemy Pass—into northern Laos. Once this had been accomplished, "massive American strikes" would destroy enemy armor and troop concentrations on the plain and allow a combined Neutralist–Hmong force to reoccupy the plain.[20] It was an ambitious plan to say the least and one that was met with well-placed skepticism by the Americans. Sullivan also cautioned against deepening U.S. involvement, which might provoke an escalating North Vietnamese response, and instead advocated a much more modest campaign of localized objectives to strengthen the government grip on the territory it now held.

Sullivan needn't have worried as General Ouane's grandiose vision failed to come to fruition. Instead government forces in the northeast and along the plain appeared to be content with engaging in small-scale skirmishing and launching limited probes into enemy territory, while they recovered and reequipped from the intense fighting earlier in the year. Even the normally aggressive Vang Pao was content to rest most of his battle-weary troops and focus on small-scale harassing operations against the enemy across Sam Neua and Xiang Khouang provinces.

The Pathet Lao and North Vietnamese, however, were more than willing to take the fight to the enemy. In the pre-dawn hours of July 16 a dozen North Vietnamese sappers

Above: By 1967 the Thai air base at Nakhon Phanom had evolved into the primary airfield for U.S. Air Force special operations squadrons operating in the Laotian theater. (Photo Museum of the U.S. Air Force)

Left: Forward air controllers, flying small planes like the O-1 Bird Dog, helped to provide critical targeting and coordination for U.S. air strikes. (Photo Museum of the U.S. Air Force)

infiltrated the airfield at Luang Prabang again and placed satchel charges and grenades on most of the RLAF T-28s there. The resulting explosions tore apart nine of the 11 planes, damaged several other aircraft, and destroyed a major portion of the ammunition dump.[21] The attack effectively reduced the size of the entire RLAF T-28 fleet by almost a quarter. The Americans pledged to replace the lost aircraft, but it would take until October for the squadron at Luang Prabang to return to full strength. In the meantime, communist forces took advantage of the situation to bring additional men and supplies into the Nam Bac valley, while also conducting a number of forays against Hmong bases and lima sites north of Route 6 in July and August.

To counter this unusual communist rainy season activity, the remaining T-28s at Luang Prabang flew constantly, but poorly organized and controlled strikes meant their bombing did little to reduce the mounting pressure on the Nam Bac garrison. To take up some of the slack, Sullivan requested the Seventh Air Force step up its efforts against enemy lines of supply and communication in the northeast. Thus, in addition to the regularly scheduled Barrel Roll interdiction missions against roads and bridges, storage depots, transshipment points, and vehicular traffic, the Air Force instituted Operation Knight Watch. The goal was to make more efficient use of diverted Air Force strike packages when poor weather conditions and low visibility over North Vietnam forced Rolling Thunder missions to be aborted. Rather than have the diverted planes simply dump their payloads over northern Laos, Skyraiders from the 602nd ACS would now serve as FACs to mark and direct more precision air strikes.

Mounting smoke rockets on an O-1E Bird Dog for marking targets. (Photo Museum of the U.S. Air Force)

The first Knight Watch mission took place on July 30 when a 47-plane strike package of F-105s and F-4 Phantoms was directed by the Skyraiders to attack the heavily defended Pathet Lao headquarters complex near Sam Neua city. No planes were lost despite the intense 37-mm and 57-mm antiaircraft fire thrown up. A post-strike assessment indicated significant damage to the complex. It would be another month before the next Knight Watch strike, but over the course of three days in late August and early September, 602nd pilots directed more than 200 aircraft against the headquarters complex, hammering the target. Two more Knight Watch strikes by nearly 100 aircraft in mid-September touched off multiple secondary explosions with fireballs rising several hundred feet in the air that ultimately reduced the complex to rumble. Against no losses, the Air Force was credited with destroying more than 100 antiaircraft weapons, 56 trucks, four storage depots, two fuel farms, two ammunition dumps, and killing over 1,800 enemy soldiers.[22]

Despite these ongoing American and Lao air operations, communist troops continued to nibble away at the Nam Bac perimeter. Critically, by September the enemy occupied most of the high ground surrounding the valley from which they could rain mortar and artillery fire down on the defenders and the airstrip. Although still too few in number

An FAC pilot keeps track of strike information and target coordinates the old fashion way. (Photo Museum of the U.S. Air Force)

to launch any meaningful attack on the heavily armed garrison, the enemy continued harassing attacks to wear down the defenders. The noose around Nam Bac was tightening.

With the end of the rains in October, preparations for the 1967/8 dry offensive began in earnest and road-watch teams in northern Laos reported seeing more heavy road and construction equipment than ever before.[23] Especially disquieting for the Americans and the government was the heightened activity along Route 19 toward Nam Bac and north of Route 6 in the Phou Pha Thi area. Unfortunately, with the Seventh Air Force redirecting its attention on slowing the flow of supplies down the Ho Chi Minh Trail only 14 percent of the daily 170 sorties was dedicated to northern Laos. Not surprisingly only 40 trucks were reported destroyed or damaged during the last three months of the year, a mere pinprick to the enemy.[24]

By December 1967 there were some 2,600 Pathet Lao and NVA troops in the Nam Bac vicinity and three more battalions from the NVA's 335th Regiment at Dien Bien Phu were being mobilized. Hunkered down behind the perimeter wire were some 4,500 men, including three full FAR mobile groups and heavy artillery. Air support was provided by the ten RLAF T-28s operating out of Luang Prabang some 55 miles away. Despite this numerical and firepower superiority, the government forces were in an increasingly desperate situation. Surrounded and isolated, the garrison was completely dependent on aerial resupply by C-47s and H-34 helicopters and the presence of several thousand refugees strained the available resources. Weak leadership, lack of an effective defense plan, and falling morale created a dangerous situation. Still the FAR General Staff did little to address the problems despite increasingly urgent pleas from American advisers to act preemptively. Nam Bac was a train wreck waiting to happen.

Air War in the Southern Panhandle

At the other end of the country the war had evolved in an entirely different direction. Since April 1965 with the approval of the Souvanna government the Americans had been conducting a sustained air interdiction campaign against the Ho Chi Minh Trail, known as Operation Steel Tiger. The initial effort was supported by RLAF T-28s and on the ground by CIA road-watch teams and by locally recruited tribesmen to launch disruptive raids on the trail.[25] Government troops also conducted periodic forays into the area, but a large North Vietnamese troop presence and the North's solid grip on the eastern side

Above: RLAF T-28s equipped with 250-pound bombs, 2.75-inch rockets, and armed with .50-caliber machine guns would give government forces a much-needed punch during combat operations.

Right: RLAF T-28s destroyed and damaged following a North Vietnamese sapper attack against Luang Prabang air base in February 1967. (Photo Museum of the U.S. Air Force)

of the panhandle prevented any meaningful offensive operations. Thus, the interdiction burden was left to the Americans and their weapon of choice—air power.

It would be a Herculean task. By the end of 1965, Group 559—the North Vietnamese unit responsible for transporting men and supplies down the trail—had grown to nearly 25,000 men, organized into eight truck and bicycle battalions, one transport boat battalion, 18 engineering battalions, four antiaircraft battalions, and numerous communication and support elements.[26] Most strikingly, the volume of supplies transported was nearly equal to the total volume of supplies transported between 1959 and 1964 and during 1965 alone almost 50,000 North Vietnamese cadre and soldiers marched south along the trail to the South Vietnamese battlefield.[27] To further increase the capacity of the Truong Son corridor (as it was known in North Vietnam) thousands of young North Vietnamese men and women volunteers were also sent in to Laos to assist in "carrying out the work of road building and maintaining the flow of traffic."[28]

The Battle For Laos: Vietnam's Proxy War 1955–1975

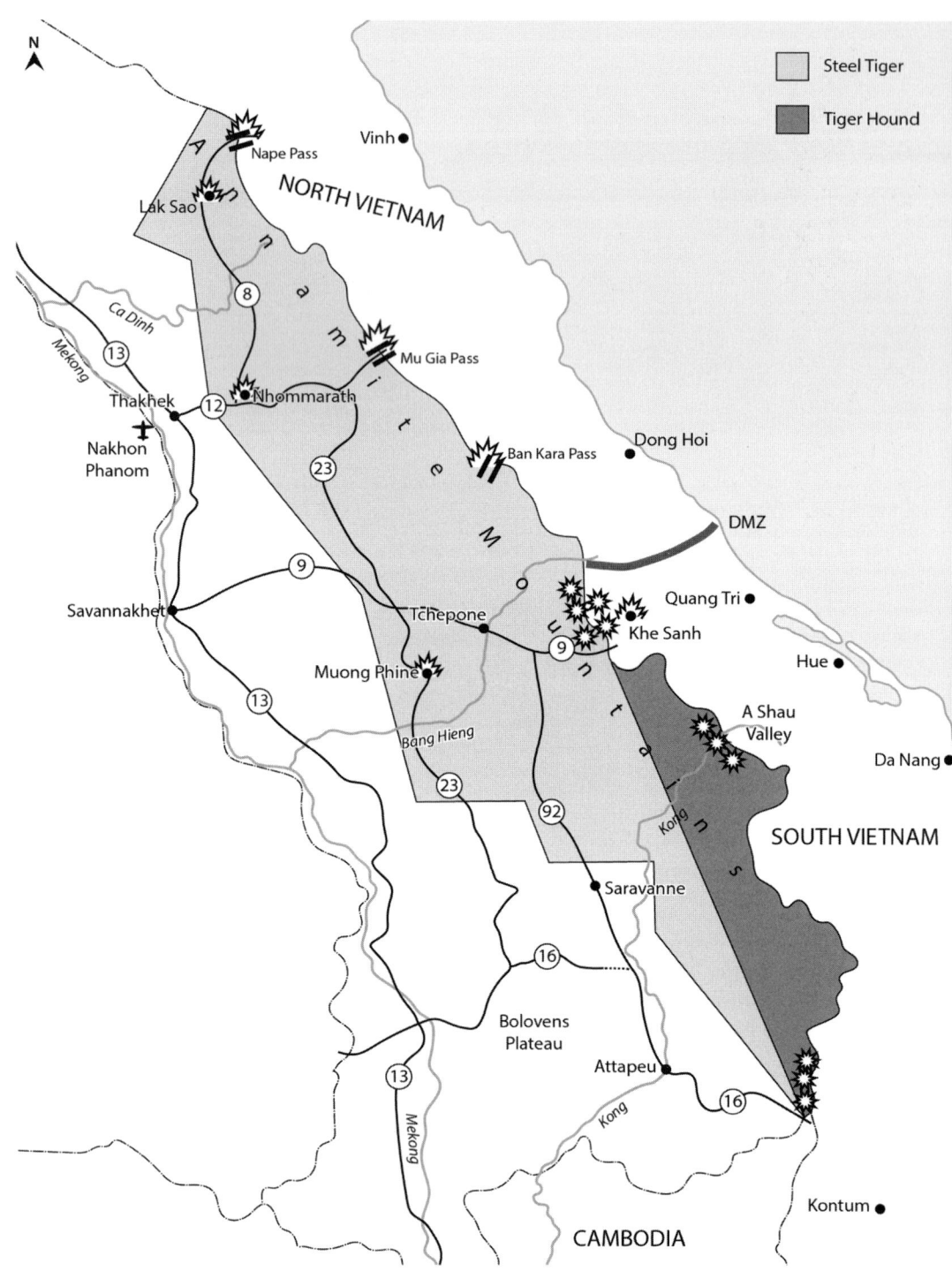

Southern Panhandle.

U.S. Air Force A-1E Skyraider armed with a Pave Pat fuel-air-explosive bomb that was used with devastating effect against enemy supply and bivouac areas along the Ho Chi Minh Trail. (Photo National Museum of the U.S. Air Force)

U.S. Air Force A-1E Skyraiders based out of Pleiku, South Vietnam, were initially tasked with supporting Lao air operations in the mid-1960s. (Photo National Museum of the U.S. Air Force)

A-1H Skyraiders of the 1st Air Commando Squadron at Nakhon Phanom air base, Thailand, in early 1968 armed and ready to go. (Photo National Museum of the U.S. Air Force)

A-1 Skyraiders with their ability to carry powerful and diverse ordnance loads—ranging from 250-pound to 1,000-pound bombs, cluster munitions, napalm, and 2.75-inch rockets—proved to be the backbone of close air support for much of the war. (Photo U.S. Air Force)

The addition of new A-7D light attack aircraft to its Thai-based inventory provided the Air Force a more robust ground-attack capability late in the war. (Photo National Museum of the U.S. Air Force)

Every fifth round a red tracer. Air Force and later Lao AC-47 gunships capable of firing 6,000 rounds per minute were often the difference in turning back communist ground assaults. (Photo National Museum of the U.S. Air Force)

Time lapse image of AC-47 providing defensive fire during the 1968 Tet Offensive. (Photo National Museum of the U.S. Air Force)

Air Force AC-47D of the 4th Air Commando Squadron based out of Nakhon Phanom air base, September 1968. (Photo National Museum of the U.S. Air Force)

AC-119G gunships utilized a black paint scheme to make them harder to detect, thus their call sign "Shadow." Photo National Museum of the U.S. Air Force)

First introduced in 1968, the AC-119s quickly became a mainstay of interdiction and close air support operations with the upgraded K versions carrying advanced detection devices, as well as two 20-mm cannons in addition to the standard four GAU 2/A miniguns. (Photo National Museum of the U.S. Air Force)

The AC-130s were the deadliest and most advanced of the Air Force's fixed-wing gunships, earning them the moniker of the "truck killers" of the Ho Chi Minh Trail. (Photo National Museum of the U.S. Air Force)

Aerial view of the much-prized and bitterly contested terrain of the Plain of Jars.

Air America UH-1 delivering supplies to a remote government outpost.

The A-26K Counter Invader was an updated version of the old World War II B-26 bomber that was heavily armed with up to 14 fixed .50-caliber machine guns and the capability to carry 4,000 pounds of armaments on eight external pylons. (Photo National Museum of the U.S. Air Force)

B-52 heavy bomber Arc Light strikes were capable of laying waste to a 2.5-square-mile area.

First used in bombing the Mu Gia Pass in December 1965, the big bombers would increasingly be called upon by 1970 to defend government positions in central Laos from being overrun. (Photo U.S. Air Force)

CIA propaganda leaflet extolling the evils of life under communist rule. (National Museum of the U.S. Air Force Archives Collection)

Above left: Forward air controller's view of an F-4 Phantom strike against a target on the Ho Chi Minh Trail. (Photo National Museum of the U.S. Air Force)

Above right: By 1969 Air Force F-4s would play an increasingly active combat role in Laos following the end of the Rolling Thunder operations in North Vietnam. (Photo U.S. Air Force)

Right: Air Force forward air controller marking a target with white phosphorus rocket for an incoming air strike. (Photo National Museum of the U.S. Air Force)

Above: Long Chieng and Lima Site 20A served as headquarters of General Vang Pao's Hmong army and operational base for CIA paramilitary efforts.

Left: CIA officer working with Lao military personnel in 1965 as part of America's "secret war." (Photo National Museum of the U.S. Air Force)

A modified C-123 Provider equipped with infrared scanner to detect nighttime activity along the Ho Chi Minh Trail. (Photo U.S. Air Force)

The North Vietnamese moved increasing numbers of antiaircraft weapons into the Laotian panhandle to counter U.S. air interdiction efforts, rising to perhaps 1,500 by the end of 1971.

A modern-day view of Phou Pha Thi Mountain, better known as Lima Site 85, and site of the costly loss of Air Force lives in ground combat during the Vietnam War.

Phou Pha Xai ridge on the southwestern edge of the Plain of Jars, part of the last defensive line of the Hmong heartland.

RF-4C of the 14th Tactical Reconnaissance Squadron takes off from Udorn, Thailand, for a mission over Laos in the late 1960s. (Photo National Museum of the U.S. Air Force)

RF-101Cs of the 45th Tactical Reconnaissance Squadron flew some of the first Yankee Team photo-reconnaissance missions over southern Laos in 1965. (Photo National Museum of the U.S. Air Force)

Above: The easy-to-fly and extremely durable T-28D became the close air support workhorse of the Royal Lao Air Force.

Left: T-28 trainers at Udorn, Thailand, as part of American training for Lao pilots under Project Water Pump that began in 1964. (Photo National Museum of the U.S. Air Force)

Air Force U-10Ds flying a propaganda leaflet drop operation over the mountainous terrain of northern Laos. (Photo National Museum of the U.S. Air Force)

Huey helicopter gunner on the hunt for enemy trucks or activity in the Laotian panhandle. (Photo U.S. Air Force)

The challenging terrain would also present another serious obstacle to air interdiction given the heavily forested and dense jungle canopy of the panhandle through which hundreds of miles of improved and rudimentary roads, twisting trails, and navigable waterways flowed. Likewise, natural barriers and chokepoints in southern Laos were few and far between and alternative routes and access points plentiful. And while the main mountain passes—Nape, Mu Gia, Ban Karai, and Ban Raving—crossing the North Vietnamese border could be temporarily blocked by large-scale bombing, they couldn't be permanently closed to traffic as an army of onsite laborers moved quickly to remove rubble, fill crater holes, and repair the roads to make them passable.

The other major obstacle for Steel Tiger was a political one: how to continue to perpetuate the myth of Lao neutrality and not undermine the Souvanna government's international position while drastically escalating American military involvement. Thus for Ambassador Sullivan, U.S. political considerations were always paramount even if this meant "bending over backwards" in executing the military mission: "American military interests should not take precedence over the need to preserve Laos's neutral status."[29] In practice this resulted in establishing complex liaison and target clearance procedures with the Laotians, as well as instituting extensive rules of engagement for U.S. pilots. Needless to say Sullivan would find himself constantly clashing with General Westmoreland over how best to find the correct balance for Steel Tiger in the wake of the building threat to South Vietnam.

Nonetheless, American pilots and aircrews would try their best to stop, or at least hinder, the flow of men and matériel into South Vietnam. Initial Steel Tiger operations relied on U.S. Air Force RF-101s and RB-57s for target detection and damage assessment, while the firepower was provided by F-100s, F-105s, and B-57s,[30] along with Navy A-4s and A-1s flying off aircraft carriers in the Gulf of Tonkin. Their primary targets were key road segments, potential chokepoints, bridges, suspected truck parks, and storage areas. At night, individual or pairs of aircraft conducted armed reconnaissance missions seeking out enemy troops and trucks moving under cover of darkness with often a flare-carrying C-130 accompanying B-57 missions. Soon Air Force and Navy pilots were flying more than 1,000 sorties per month over the Ho Chi Minh Trail with this number rising to almost 3,000 by the end of 1965.[31]

The main routes leading from the Mu Gia and Nape passes were a high priority from the start. Seven B-57s took part in the initial bombing of Mu Gia Pass on April 4 while Air Force and Navy aircraft cratered nearby roads in the days following. By mid-July

General William Momyer, commander of the Seventh Air Force in Thailand. (Photo U.S. Air Force)

1965 a typical F-105 air strike would see 18,000 pounds of ordnance being released on each of these two passes and the first use of B-52s in Laos would also be against Mu Gia Pass on December 11.[32] Some of the first Steel Tiger air losses would be here too: an Air Force Thunderchief out of Takhil on April 17 and a Navy Skyraider off the USS *Hancock* on April 27.[33] They would not be the last.

The other priority interdiction area for the Americans was the southernmost section of Laotian panhandle adjoining the South Vietnamese border, which was designated Operation *Tiger Hound* in December 1965. Using enhanced reconnaissance flights, low-flying O-1 Bird Dog FACs, C-130 flare ships, defoliation-spraying UC-123s, and on-the-ground intelligence-gathering teams, General Westmoreland and MACV hope to concentrate more air strikes here as part of his "extended battlefield" approach to the war in South Vietnam. The effort steadily gained momentum by early 1966 with tactical air strikes claiming the destruction of hundreds of trucks, while B-52 bombers flew more than 400 Arc Light strikes—massive saturation bombing of a one-and-a-half-mile-long by half-a-mile-wide area—in the first half of 1966.[34] By June, U.S. commanders were claiming to have destroyed or damaged an estimated 3,000 structures, 1,400 trucks, scores of bridges, and more than 200 antiaircraft positions in the southern panhandle.[35]

Yet still the North Vietnamese not only kept the trail open, but continued to work feverishly throughout 1966 to expand their logistics capacity. By the end of the year they had built a startling vehicle-capable road network of 1,850 miles to support five transportation battalions consisting of nearly 5,400 trucks. This would allow Group 559 to move a total of 61,000 tons of supplies during the upcoming 1967/8 dry season, which would be more than double the previous year's effort.[36] Group 599 also facilitated the buildup of combat forces in the South, which would rise to 230,000 men by the end of 1966.[37] To protect these operations against air attack increasing numbers of antiaircraft weapons and air defense units were dispatched to the panhandle, accounting for the loss of 52 American planes—including three AC-47s and two A-26Ks—and the deaths of 56 pilots and crew since the start of the air campaign.[38]

CIA road-watch teams working deep behind enemy lines provided valuable intelligence on communist activity in northeastern Laos, as well as along the Ho Chi Minh Trail.

Raising the Stakes

To counter this rising challenge the U.S. sortie rate over the panhandle rose dramatically to a monthly peak of 3,400 in early 1967.[39] This increase was accompanied by a sharp rise in large-scale operations—known as SLAM (Seek, Locate, Annihilate, and Monitor) missions—in the *Tiger Hound* operational area. Using special operations teams airlifted inside Laos, suspected targets were pinpointed and then subjected to massive American bombing. Several large supply complexes and staging areas opposite Kontum Province and the A Shau Valley were hit repeatedly by SLAM strikes. In one instance east of the A Shau Valley, the Air Force flew 1,526 combat sorties with B-52s contributing another 256 Arc Light strikes over a period of two weeks in mid-February 1967 that touched off hundreds of secondary explosions and killed nearly 200 of the enemy.[40] For political reasons the SLAM strikes were strictly confined to a 12-mile target zone across the South Vietnamese border.

In addition, General Momyer wanted to up the operations tempo across the panhandle by using nighttime B-52 strikes against the trail that would be interspersed with tactical air

Right: As part of General Westmoreland's extended battlefield, various American specialized units began regularly operating across the border into Laos. (Photo Museum of the U.S. Air Force)

Below: The heavily armed A-26K Counter Invader was a key element of early Steel Tiger interdiction efforts in the Laotian panhandle.

strikes during the day to create and maintain critical chokepoints. Ambassador Sullivan, however, was reluctant to open up large parts of Steel Tiger to more frequent and intense bombing, especially by B-52s. He argued that the negative political repercussions for the Souvanna government—allowing the Americans to conduct a widespread and highly visible bombing campaign in his officially neutral country—far outweighed the potential military benefits. Instead he believed that smaller, but more numerous armed reconnaissance missions supported by an increased airborne FAC presence would be more effective and pose less political risk. To support his case, Sullivan pointed to the highly successful A-26K program. By March 1967, the Counter Invaders had had flown some 2,000 sorties over the previous seven months and were credited with 1,233 attacks that destroyed or damaged 521 trucks, 47 gun positions, 823 bivouac areas, and killed nearly 500 troops.[41]

Perhaps one of the more profound developments in the air war was the establishment of a Steel Tiger task force at Nakhon Phanom in March 1967. Its mission was to better coordinate the activities of intelligence collection and interdiction units at the base, including the 56th Air Commando Wing, the 23rd Tactical Air Support Squadron, and the tactical unit operations center of the 432nd Tactical Reconnaissance Wing. Over time the task force became quite adept at diverting strike aircraft to suddenly discovered truck parks, supply depots, and other transitory targets.[42] By July, however, the task force would be supplanted by more direct air-to-ground communications networks that bypassed Nakhon Phanom and that would eventually be merged with a new center testing air-supported anti-infiltrations systems in late 1967. This new endeavor would evolve into the Infiltration Surveillance Center, which was to play a central role in American interdiction efforts from 1968 onward.

For all this progress, old problems over complex rules of engagement and targeting, along with unresolved tensions over the nature and control of air operations between

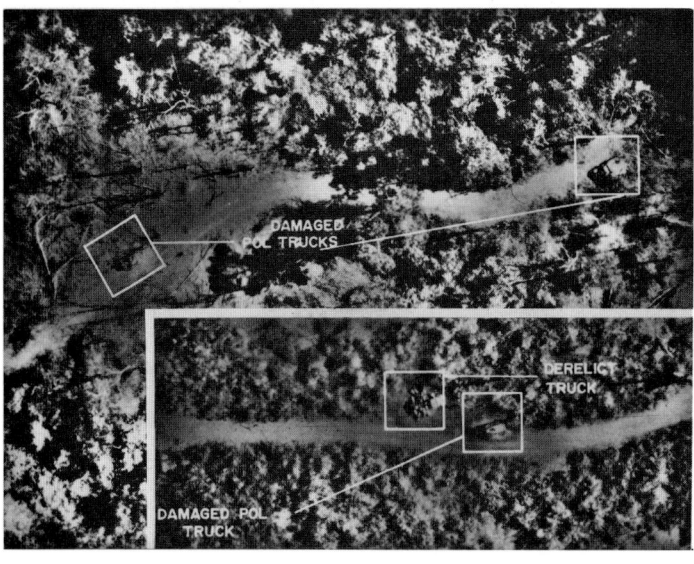

Remnants of a North Vietnamese fuel truck convoy struck by American aircraft in Savannakhet Province, December 1967. (Photo U.S. Air Force)

military commanders and the U.S. Embassy in Vientiane continued to dog the interdiction effort in southern Laos.

One continuing major source of tension was over the proper role and use of B-52 bombers in the panhandle. While Ambassador Sullivan and State Department analysts were far from convinced as to the effectiveness of Arc Light strikes as an interdiction tool and the Embassy was acutely aware of the domestic and international sensitivities involved in their use, military commanders were all in. General Westmoreland, who called the SAC operations indispensable for interdiction, pressed Washington for a 50-percent increase in B-52 sorties with much of this increase directed at the Laotian panhandle.[43] Pointing to the recent success of Arc Light saturation bombing of the DMZ in the spring of 1967, which reportedly killed more than 3,600 enemy soldiers, Westmoreland said, "there is every reason to believe ... the B-52 has become and will continue to be a decisive weapon for destroying staging and logistic areas and disrupting enemy [troop] concentrations."[44] Westmoreland got his way thanks in part to a Thai agreement to allow the stationing of 25 B-52s and supporting KC-135 tankers at U-Tapao air base. The newly enlarged bomber fleet in Thailand would be able to supply 800 monthly sorties with the Guam-based aircraft supplying the remaining 400 monthly sorties. The Thai-based bombers flew their first missions on December 30 against Lao and South Vietnamese targets. This would come none too soon, because less than a month later the North Vietnamese caught the Americans off guard, not in Laos, but rather in South Vietnam when they launched the largest military offensive of the war yet: the January 31, 1968 Tet Offensive.

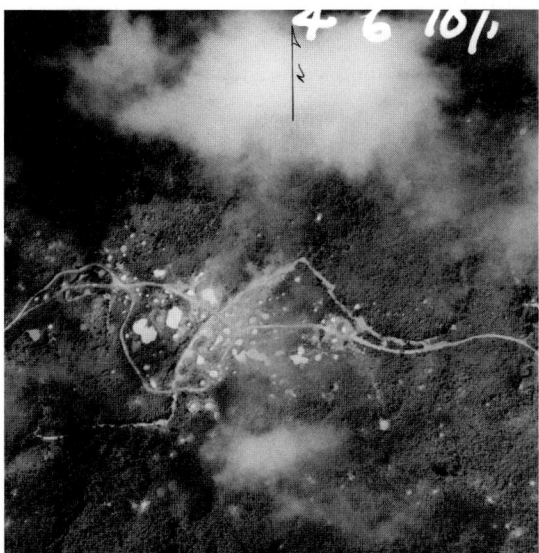

Above left: Bridge interdiction efforts were a key element of early Steel Tiger operations. (Photo Museum of the U.S. Air Force)

Above right: Air Force B-52 bombers out of Guam struck Mu Gia Pass for the first time in December 1965. (Photo Museum of the U.S. Air Force)

5. ESCALATION

Just as the war in South Vietnam was building toward a climax in the late 1960s, the more than decade-long conflict in Laos was about to undergo dramatic changes too. The fighting would become more deadly, more expansive, and constantly threatening to engulf both Washington and Hanoi in a greater confrontation neither wanted, yet each would find hard to avoid when push came to shove. Nonetheless, both still continued to pursue policies of military brinksmanship when they believed the survival of their Lao allies or their own interests were at stake.

The Northern Battlefield: Round Three

Declining government fortunes on the battlefield at the end of 1967 culminated in early 1968 with two major defeats at the hands of North Vietnamese troops, who were now at the forefront of nearly all communist military operations in Laos. With the exception of airlifting 880 men of Mobile Group 15 out of Nam Bac on December 23 and having Lao T-28s continuing to bomb the besieging enemy forces, little was being done to rectify a worsening military situation. The inevitable came on January 14 with an assault by some 1,600 men of the NVA's 335th Regiment that crushed any semblance of resistance. Broken and demoralized, the government troops scattered; it was everyman for himself. For several months afterward stragglers drifted into Vang Pao's forward base at Muong Ngoi, but only 1,500 of the more than 3,600 men were ever accounted for. Likewise, equipment losses were staggering: nearly $1.3 million in supplies abandoned, including seven 105-mm howitzers, 33,000 artillery shells, and over a million rounds of small-arms ammunition.[1]

Compounding this disaster was the loss of Lima Site 85 atop Phou Pha Thi—a covert navigation and radar site in northern Laos that provided all-weather bombing capability for Rolling Thunder strikes—a few months later in March, which was soon followed by the forced evacuation of nearly all remaining Hmong enclaves in Sam Neua Province. The loss of Phou Pha Thi was especially painful for both the Americans and Vang Pao. Not only did it mean the loss of a vital installation that would be difficult to replace, but it was a major psychological blow to the Hmong general's prestige. To exacerbate Vang Pao's problems, communist forces also began a systematic effort to cleanse the region of Hmong guerrillas. Five more lima sites were overrun by April and the targeting of Hmong villagers and their crops precipitated a mass refugee exodus. Thousands of guerrillas and their families were airlifted by Air America to safety, but tens of thousands more were forced to trek nearly 250 miles across the war-torn landscape before finding refuge. By mid-year more than 150,000 Hmong had fled the northeast.

As the North Vietnamese-led communist offensive gained steam, only the Hmong base at Na Khang and LS 36 remained standing as the last government bastion in the northeast.

The Battle for Lima Site 85

In early 1968 a remote secret outpost high atop a mountain peak in northern Laos would become the scene for the largest ground combat loss of the U.S. Air Force personnel during the Vietnam War.

As the American bombing campaign against North Vietnam, known as Operation Rolling Thunder, gained momentum in 1967 there developed a glaring need to provide advanced technical support for U.S. air operations over Hanoi and Haiphong during the northeast monsoon. From October to April poor target visibility often limited air strikes to all-weather attack aircraft like the Navy's A-6 Intruder, of which there were only a few squadrons in the Southeast Asian theater. The Air Force's F-105s—the mainstay of their strike force—were reduced to flying missions on the four or five days a month of clear weather. Something needed to be done.

The proposed solution required installing modified guidance radar, the TSQ-81, to provide targeting data to pilots and enable them to drop their bombs solely on instrument readings. The system, however, required a location that provided an unobstructed line of sight to the target area and one that also had to be within 175 miles of the targets. Lima Site 85 fit the bill perfectly. Sitting atop the 5,580-foot Phou Pha Thi Mountain, it was only 15 miles from the North Vietnamese border and had an unobstructed view of the Red River valley all the way to Hanoi some 160 miles to the east. Nonetheless, there were serious drawbacks. It sat deep within enemy territory and was only about 20 miles west of the Pathet Lao headquarters at Sam Neua and could only be resupplied by small aircraft and helicopters.

The Air Force's need outweighed the risk and in late October 1967 Air Force CH-47 cargo helicopters transported the TSQ-81 radar and other supporting communications equipment to the site. It went operational on November 1 and soon proved its worth, directing 13 percent of Rolling Thunder strikes in November and 55 percent by February as the weather over the North worsened. The site was staffed and supported by 48 Air Force personnel of the 1st Combat Evaluations Group out of Udorn, Thailand. All the men involved were volunteers who had been "sheep dipped" as part of the covert program known as *Heavy Green*. Officially they had all "resigned" from the Air Force and were hired on as Lockheed contract employees as part of a government contract to maintain and repair communications facilities in Laos. They all wore civilian clothes and carried Lockheed identification cards. Security was afforded by the sheer face of the mountain with cliffs on three sides and the fourth heavily fortified and protected some 200 Hmong and Thai fighters. Another 800 men were arrayed around the base of the mountain to provide defense in depth.

By the middle of February 1968 an estimated 3,000 Pathet Lao and North Vietnamese troops were closing in on the mountain and the CIA warned that the position could not be held beyond mid-March. To break up the enemy advance during the final week in February the Air Force flew an unprecedented 342 sorties, but still the encirclement of Phou Pha Thi continued.

On March 10, there were 19 Americans at the site, including 16 *Heavy Green* personnel, when the encircling forces unleashed an early evening artillery and rocket barrage.

Shortly thereafter, communist troops engaged the Hmong defenders at the base of the mountain and throughout the night A-26Ks and F-4s repeatedly struck the attackers, but the situation was becoming critical. Although Air Force officials resisted, Ambassador Sullivan finally decided to evacuate the site the next morning.

Just before midnight on March 10, 33 North Vietnamese sappers climbed the sheer cliff side of the western side of the mountain, a feat the Americans thought impossible. They emerged at the top of the mountain, hiding until the early morning hours of March 11 before moving toward the *Heavy Green* facilities. Following an accidently encounter with a Hmong soldier, an intense firefight broke out with the sappers firing on the radar buildings with rocket-propelled grenades and submachine guns, taking the Americans there by surprise. The attackers also discovered a group of Americans taking refuge from the earlier bombardment on a rock overhang below the mountaintop and began firing down on them and lobbing grenades. Several Americans on the ledge were killed outright and several others were seriously wounded. Chief Master Sargent Richard Etchberger, however, was unhurt and began returning fire with his M-16 rifle and was able to keep the attackers at bay.

The arriving evacuation helicopters found themselves under heavy small-arms fire from the summit that kept them from landing. A CIA officer and several Hmong and Thai soldiers, however, were able to maneuver up to the *Heavy Green* facilities from their base below and engage the attackers. In an ensuing firefight, the CIA officer was wounded and several Hmong soldiers were killed. Just in the nick of time a flight of A-1s arrived to strafe the enemy, allowing the circling helicopters to approach the site.

An Air America Huey spotted Etchberger and the wounded men on the ledge and the flight engineer brought them up with by cable. Etchberger remained until all the wounded and one other surviving technician were aboard before being hoisted up. No sooner was he inside the helicopter than he was struck by ground fire and mortally wounded. For his actions Richard Etchberger would be posthumously awarded the Air Force Cross for bravery. In 2010 the award was upgraded to the Medal of Honor.

Throughout the morning Air America and Air Force helicopters shuttled into the base of the mountain extracted the remaining Americans and wounded defenders. Badly outnumbered now, the Hmong defenders began to withdraw into the jungle and soon Phou Pha Thi fell completely to the enemy. To avoid having this sensitive equipment fall into enemy hands, Air Force planes completely leveled the site.

Escalation

> Of the 19 Americans, eight were accounted for, eight were confirmed dead, and three missing presumed dead. In their report of the battle, the North Vietnamese claimed to have killed 42 and wounded many more. There was no mention of dead Americans. All the *Heavy Green* survivors and those airmen killed during the battle were officially "restored" to the Air Force, but it would be another 30 years before the full story of the battle became public.

Vang Pao reinforced the garrison to bring its total to some 1,500 by late April and CIA officers on the ground worked with the Seventh Air Force to coordinate a defense. On May 5 the assault by some 1,500 North Vietnamese and Pathet Lao troops began with attacks on two outlying outposts. Both were quickly overrun, forcing Vang Pao to request "max air [support]," including the use of napalm.² The response was almost immediate with 17 Skyraiders from the 602nd Fighter Commando Squadron out of Nakhon Phanom joining orbiting F-105s and F-4s to rain destruction down on the advancing enemy. Time after time the attackers regrouped only to be bombed again. The American air assault continued over the course of the next two days with Vang Pao often riding along with a Ravan FAC to personally direct strikes and coordinate ground operations. "We literally pulverized the place and they finally retreated [on May 8]," recalled an American adviser.³ But there was no letup in the American air strikes as counterattacking Hmong fighters nipped at the heels of the retreating enemy. By May 13 the Air Force had flown nearly 300 sorties, helping to wipe out nearly the entire attacking force of some four battalions.⁴ Na Khang had been saved, at least for now.

But the communists were not quite done. On May 20 a reserve force of four enemy battalions was brought up to continue the attack, but the Americans were ready with 60 planned defensive air sorties. The renewed assault never got going in the face of this pressure and by May 27 the communists abandoned the siege and withdrew completely from the area. A jubilant Ambassador Sullivan cabled General Momyer and the Seventh Air Force to express his deepest appreciation for the excellent response in the defense of Na Khang.

Now it was Vang Pao's turn. Despite resistance from his American advisers, the general was bent on launching a rainy season offensive in the northeast and the recapture of LS 85 would be the crowning jewel. His reputation was on the line, as well as his standing among the Hmong who considered the mountain a sacred place. Eventually the Americans gave in and on June 27 airlifted 750 of his fighters to a position outside of Muong Son, about 15 miles west of Phou Pha Thi and LS 85. Once seizing Muong Son and its airfield, Vang Pao hoped to fly in additional reinforcements for the advance on Phou Pha Thi. Unexpectedly the Hmong troops encountered stiff enemy resistance at Muong Son and were forced to call upon air power with the Air Force flying nearly 300 sorties over the next two weeks. This did the trick and Muong Son and its airfield were taken on July 22.

With the element of surprise lost and almost a month behind schedule, Vang Pao now found himself and his men at Muong Son facing a series of enemy counterattacks and harassing artillery fire. Hunkered down in their defenses the Hmong battalions called in air strikes to keep the enemy at bay throughout the summer. In the meantime, intelligence sources were reporting an extensive buildup of more than 16 NVA battalions in the Sam Neua area and possible preparations for an early dry-season offensive.[5]

Not one to be easily discouraged, Vang Pao embarked on a new plan. He would strike directly at Phou Pha Thi at a time when the communists least expected it— at the start of the dry season. With pledges of extensive American air support and the opportunity to disrupt Pathet Lao and North Vietnamese planning, the general launched Operation Pig Fat with some 1,500 men in late November.

An American Skyraider pulls up after delivering its payload against the enemy. (Photo Museum of the U.S. Air Force)

The enemy troops were caught completely off guard. One enemy position after the other fell to the advancing Hmong troops and by early December they had reached LS 107 at Ban Cha Thao on the main approach to Phou Pha Thi. Here they established an artillery fire support base to pound the mountain with 105-mm howitzer fire. Unfortunately, weather delays prevented Barrel Roll air strikes from catching the reported NVA troop concentration near Sam Neua, but the enemy defenders on Phou Pha Thi soon found themselves subject to an unrelenting barrage of rockets, bombs, and napalm by Air Force and RLAF planes. Overcoming fierce resistance, the Hmong troops reached the helipad and the mountain summit by December 18. However, elsewhere on the mountain the North Vietnamese remained dug in and a series of counterattacks on Christmas Day seemed to turn the tide. Once the NVA's 148th Regiment overran the fire support base at LS 107 on January 3, Vang Pao was forced to begin pulling his men off the mountain and fall back toward Na Khang.

Although Operation Pig Fat had failed to retake LS 85, it did successfully disrupt and delay the planned communist dry-season offensive and inflict significant casualties on the enemy at a small cost. Vang Pao reported his forces suffered 40 dead and 131 wounded, while a number of North Vietnamese units were decimated by air strikes. One North Vietnamese prisoner reported that half of his battalion was killed by air attacks, less than 400 of the 1,200 communist defenders on Phou Pha Thi survived, and the 148th Regiment suffered 128 killed and 250 wounded.[6]

Escalation

Above: The embattled garrison at Bouam Long was able to hold out despite repeated communist assaults thanks in large part to the withering defensive fire provided by AC-47 gunships.

Left: A CIA paramilitary adviser on the Plain of Jars looks on as a Hmong officer communicates with headquarters.

The Northern Battlefield: Round Four

Bloodied, but not dissuaded, the North Vietnamese-spearheaded 1968/9 dry-season offensive got off to a start with a familiar objective: Na Khang. Although now only lightly defended, Vang Pao was confident he could hold the position by rushing in reinforcements and relying once again on air power to save the day. After all it had worked before. A lot, however, had changed over the course of eight months. The Hmong army was battered and exhausted, its ranks depleted after non-stop fighting and suffering from low morale after recent setbacks. More important, the North Vietnamese commanders had taken to heart the hard lessons of last year's assault and changed their tactics. No more massing of troops to create lucrative targets for air strikes. No more frontal assaults against fortified positions with covering firepower. Dispersion and concealment were now the name of the game.

Using just three battalions from the newly arrived 316th Division, the North Vietnamese began closing in on Na Khang and LS 36 at the end of February 1969. On the 28th they launched their first probing attacks, quickly capturing several outposts. Immediate calls for air support brought in American aircraft that struck all around the perimeter, but apparently inflicted few casualties on the well-dispersed enemy. Just as the battle was beginning to take shape a chance mortar round hit the base command post on the night of March 1, killing the Hmong commander and most of his officers. Leaderless and demoralized the garrison's troops took flight. The North Vietnamese soldiers walked into base unopposed the next day.

Just like that a key symbol of Hmong resistance over the past three years was no more. The loss of Na Khang and other sites in the northeast was noteworthy for the relative ease in which Vang Pao's troops collapsed, signaling an army of the verge of collapse. In one case, a defensive position was reportedly left in the hands of recruits as young as 12 years old. This prompted one CIA officer to say that "if you wanted the Hmong to fight, you had to count on children to do it."[7] Even more worrisome, the route to the Muong Soui and Hmong heartland at Long Chieng was now completely vulnerable, protected only by a lightly defended crescent of three lima sites. Moreover, the communists appeared to have ample time and forces to make their move against either of these objectives before the end of the dry season. The loss of either Long Chieng or Muong Soui would likely spell disaster and "seriously shake the fragile government" to its knees, according to the U.S. Embassy.[8] The war was on the verge of a turning point. Souvanna knew it. The Americans knew it.

However, as fate would have it a North Vietnamese defector disclosed that the main line of advance would be toward Muong Soui with an opening assault spearheaded by the 924th Regiment on the lima site crescent on March 23. Well aware that these sites would not be able to withstand such a determined attack and of the need to rebuild morale, Vang Pao pushed for an all-out offensive against the Plain of Jars to disrupt the enemy plans. Although Souvanna approved the idea, American officials in Vientiane thought the plan "completely impractical" given the state of Vang Pao's forces and that it smacked as "an act of desperation reminiscent of the last German counteroffensive in the winter of 1944."[9] Instead the Embassy proposed a three-day air campaign, codenamed Rain Dance, against enemy transshipment points, base camps, storage facilities, and command and control installations on the eastern edge of the plain that heretofore had been off limits. To further divert the enemy's attention and reinforce the illusion of a widespread government ground offensive, Vang Pao's troops would launch a series of harassing

Vang Pao's headquarters at Long Chieng and its associated air facilities served as a forward operating airfield for Lao and American aircraft. (Photo Museum of the U.S. Air Force)

attacks toward routes 4 and 7. The simple goal of the operation was to buy time and hope the rains came in time to bog down the communist advance on Muong Soui.

Rain Dance kicked off on March 17 with some five dozen air strikes. The results were stunning and far surpassed anything the Americans and the Laotians could have anticipated. Although only seven targets were hit on the first day, the strikes resulted in hundreds of secondary explosions as large stockpiles of ammunition and fuel went up in flames. The Pathet Lao and North Vietnamese had been caught flatfooted, because the targeted areas had been off limits previously and were neither well-camouflaged nor protected against air attack. As the impressive results continued, the Air Force decided to extend the campaign. In just over a week, American aircraft had flown 261 Rain Dance sorties, causing 486 secondary explosions and igniting 244 fires, destroying 570 structures, 28 bunkers, and numerous artillery and gun positions.[10] By the time Rain Dance was over on April 7, 80 percent of the 345 targets had been completely wiped out at the cost of four American aircraft.[11]

The ground phase of the operation saw 1,500 troops launching multiple probes into the Plain of Jars on March 23. Confused and disoriented by the ongoing bombing, the Pathet Lao forces on the plain pulled back into the safety of the larger cities that had yet to be hit. Encountering little resistance, the government probes turned into major thrusts with Vang Pao's men seizing Phu Khe, about 11 miles southwest of Xieng Khouangville, and threatening to cut Route 4 by the end of the month. Meanwhile, the attack against the lima site crescent to the north of the plain got underway in mid-April with an assault on Bouam Long (LS 32) by three Pathet Lao battalions. Aided by newly deployed RLAF AC-47

An F-4 Phantom laying down close air support. (Photo Museum of the U.S. Air Force)

gunships and U.S tactical jets, the crusty old Hmong warrior, Moua Cher Pao, and his men decimated the Pathet Lao troops. A second assault by elements of the NVA's 924th Regiment also failed to dislodge the defenders and helped "inject new spirit into Vang Pao's bedraggled troops everywhere."[12]

With the enemy slow to react to his advance, Vang Pao pushed even deeper into the Plain of Jars. Xieng Khouangville fell on April 29, the first time government forces had occupied the provincial capital since 1962. Ban Ban on the eastern edge was temporarily seized, as was much of the territory southeast of routes 4 and 72. Vast amounts of supplies were also captured. This situation finally forced the enemy to begin shifting forces away from the advance on Muong Soui and toward Vang Pao's position at Xieng Khouangville. In the face of this enemy buildup the general decided to withdraw from the town and surrounding area in mid-May. To help cover his withdrawal another five-day air campaign got underway to interdict Route 7. Like Rain Dance the operation scored impressive results, destroying large amounts of supplies and fuel, but it failed to halt the flow of enemy reinforcements.

By the end of May, the battle lines had reverted to their mid-March status. While the communists had regained control over nearly all the ground they lost in Rain Dance, Vang Pao accomplished his goal of halting the enemy advance on Muong Soui. Once again air power had proved decisive. Between November 1968 and May 1969 the Air Force had flown more than 11,000 sorties in Barrel Roll—more than double the previous year—and RLAF sorties also nearly doubled as well to 9,818.[13] However, it was also becoming increasingly apparent that without this high level of support little could be done by the weakened government ground troops to halt any future determined communist offensives. Fortunately, the rains had arrived and all assumed the threat was over for now.

The enemy, however, had a different idea. For the first time in the war, communist forces embarked on a wet-season offensive—Campaign Total Victory—on June 18, catching the Americans and their Lao allies completely off guard. Taking advantage of the poor weather that hampered air operations, NVA soldiers bypassed the stubborn lima site crescent line and thrust directly toward Muong Soui. Within a week three battalions of about 1,300 men from the 165th Regiment of the 312th Division and other supporting elements were outside the city after pushing the Neutralist troops off Phou Kout and from other outlying outposts.

On June 24 the North Vietnamese launched their main assault that was supported by six PT-76 light tanks. Although the Neutralist defenders vastly outnumbered the attackers

Escalation

Vang Pao (center) discusses developments with CIA officers during Operation About Face, September 1969. (Photo Museum of the U.S. Air Force)

by three to one, the leaderless and demoralized troops put up a shaky defense and began to waver. Only withering 105-mm howitzer fire from a volunteer Thai artillery battalion and the resistance from a handful of Hmong troops kept the attackers at bay as the day wore on. Just as their position was about to be overrun, a break in the weather over the battlefield allowed more than three dozen aircraft, including 14 American A-1s and 29 RLAF T-28s, to unleash bombs, rockets, and 20-mm cannon on the enemy and stop the attack in its tracks.

Despite suffering only very light casualties—two dead and 64 wounded—the Neutralists had had enough. They began to desert their positions that night even as covering AC-47 gunships and jets broke up renewed enemy attacks. By June 26 only 500 Neutralist soldiers remained alongside the Thai artillery men and the Hmong soldiers. With the writing on the wall, the decision was made to evacuate Muong Soui, just as the North Vietnamese renewed the assault with their remaining tanks. Clearing weather once again permitted aircraft to pummel the attackers with Air America and Air Force helicopters covering the withdrawal. Muong Soui fell later that evening.

To rectify the situation, the Embassy pushed General Ouane to transfer FAR troops from other military regions, but he refused because the regional commanders "would never permit it."[14] Nonetheless, an irrepressible Vang Pao proposed to recapture the city with a hastily assembled mixed force of 1,600 men that would advance under an

General Vang Pao poses by a camouflaged North Vietnamese truck damaged and captured during Operation About Face, August–September 1969. (Photo Museum of the U.S. Air Force)

air umbrella. The effort got underway on July 1. Backed by some 50 Air Force air strikes on enemy positions, 600 Hmong soldiers made good progress—without any support by other government troops—in advancing to within three miles of the city by July 5. Deteriorating weather, however, limited further American air support, so Vang Pao called on his "flying artillery" of Hmong T-28 pilots. One of those responding was Ly Lue, one of the most experienced and valiant Hmong pilots, who pressed the attack with bombs and 20-mm cannon fire against intense enemy ground fire. It would cost him his life.[15] Without support from the 1,000 Neutralist and FAR troops, who refused to join in on the attack, Vang Pao was forced to withdraw. The counterattack had failed.

While the Souvanna government and the Americans contemplated their next move, the North Vietnamese were already busy reinforcing their forces at Muong Soui, even going so far as to strip troops from other sectors. During the first two weeks of July more than 1,000 enemy trucks were reported heading westward toward Muong Soui as part of this buildup. On July 13 some of these newly arrived reinforcements along with tanks and heavy artillery then launched an assault on Vang Pao's position south of the city, driving the remaining battle-weary Hmong troops back across the Ngum River. The North Vietnamese were now firmly in control of the western edge of the plain. Moreover, there was little left now in the government's arsenal to stop the enemy.

Since the fall of Muong Soui, Prime Minister Souvanna had been pushing the Americans to help him send a powerful message to the communists. To his end, he requested an air armada of 150 American aircraft hit the Pathet Lao headquarters and main supply depot at Khang Khay that theretofore had been off limits for political reasons. Although ultimately turned down, the request resurrected old tensions within the U.S. government over Lao policy and the war in northern Laos. The State Department saw its mandate as ensuring the political survival of the Souvanna government and was willing to use every tool available (short of the introduction of American ground troops) to prevent a communist takeover. For those in the American military, however, northern Laos was but a holding action and justified the use of military assets only as a way of placating Souvanna for prosecuting the air war in the Laotian panhandle. The south was the key, not the north of the country. Thus nothing should be done elsewhere to goad Hanoi into increasing its military activity and further complicating U.S. efforts to achieve its objectives in the panhandle.

Meanwhile the strategic situation in the country had gone from bad to worse for the Souvanna government.

Beginning in 1967 the Air Force began deploying airdropped acoustic and seismic sensors to detect North Vietnamese movements along the Ho Chi Minh Trail. (Photo Museum of the U.S. Air Force)

Intelligence reports were indicating that by stripping their rear areas of combat troops, the enemy had massed nearly 8,000 men, 60 tanks, and several thousand support personnel in the Muong Soui area, while another seven battalions were concentrated in the Xieng Khouangville area.[16] This array included the battle-hardened 316th Division, as well as three infantry battalions and armor recently arrived from North Vietnam. The apparent plan was for these forces to first drive west from Muong Soui to cut Route 13 between Vientiane and Luang Prabang, before turning south to seize the main Neutralist headquarters at Vang Vieng. This maneuver would allow the enemy to outflank Vang Pao's headquarters and main base at Long Chieng, southwest of the plain, while another joint North Vietnamese–Pathet Lao force would drive down Route 54 to complete the encirclement of the Hmong heartland. If successful, the war could be lost and the Souvanna government toppled.

Critically, by pulling troops from their rear areas, the communists had left a huge vacuum stretching from the Plain of Jars back to Sam Neua and Nong Het. All that was left now across vast parts of central Laos was a sprinkling of Pathet Lao and dissident Neutralist troops, who were expected to garrison the area and support the supply network. By building up their forces so far forward in anticipation of a decisive dry-season offensive, the North Vietnamese were likely calculating that the government forces were too weak after months of continuous fighting to significantly hinder their plans.

With few palatable options available to assist the Souvanna government in light of the self-imposed American political restraints, the new U.S. ambassador, G. McMurtrie Godley, turned to air power to save the day. Godley directed the Embassy air attaché and the CIA chief of station to devise "a saturation air campaign" based on the Rain Dance model with the Seventh Air Force.[17] Thus, Operation About Face was born. It was to be an

Ground crew at Nakhon Phanom air base loading up seismic detection sensors in preparation for an Igloo White mission over the panhandle. (Photo Museum of the U.S. Air Force)

expanded version of the successful Operation Rain Dance campaign and called for 200 sorties a day to interdict Route 7 between Ban Ban and Nong Pet, armed reconnaissance flights along the roads leading to Ban Ban from North Vietnam, and the destruction of enemy supply depots across the Plain of Jars. The interdiction effort would be accomplished by creating a series of chokepoints along the 15-mile stretch from Ban Ban to Nong Pet using 2,000-pound laser-guided bombs and Bullpup missiles to break up the road surface and crater the ground. Heavy rains would then wash away the weakened roadbed and render the road impassable. Other aircraft would sow the target area with delayed-action bombs and anti-personnel mines to block repair efforts. To further hinder enemy resupply efforts, irregular guerrilla forces would move from the north and south to launch harassing attacks against repair crews or efforts to bypass the damage road segments.

A follow-on ground phase would then apply pressure on the southern edge of the plain, while other troops would maintain pressure in the Muong Soui area. Given Vang Pao's weak troop strength—the Hmong having suffered about 70 percent of government casualties in the recent fighting—the plan did not call for the retaking of Muong Soui or other towns on the plain. Disruption of the enemy buildup was the name of the game, not the occupation of territory.

But Vang Pao had other ideas. With the use of massive American air strikes, he saw the opportunity to achieve a great victory "that would demoralize Hanoi" by moving the largest possible force onto the Plain of Jars where the North Vietnamese never expected to lose a conventional battle.[18] To assist him the Embassy arranged to equip six of his best battalions with M-16 rifles and the FAR also agreed to send reinforcements from southern Laos to beef up his attacking force. Nonetheless, he would undertake the ambitious effort with just shy of 4,000 ground troops. The air assault was to start on July 15 with the ground operation beginning on the 24th. Record rains, however, delayed the start of ground operations for nearly a month, but the delay proved fortuitous in allowing the full weight of the air assault to take its toll on the enemy.

Although poor weather forced the scrubbing of some strike missions, the adoption of new all-weather bombing techniques—such as ground-directed targeting, radar bombing, and FAC-employed radar guidance—contributed to a high sortie rate: more than 4,000 during the first 30 days of the campaign.[19] The results were equally impressive—nearly 2,000 structures were destroyed, more than 1,000 secondary explosions reported, 45 anti-aircraft positions were knocked out, and 320 road cuts were created.[20] The addition of three Air Force AC-130s gunships for the first time in northern Laos also proved to be a deterrent to nighttime vehicular traffic by destroying 63 trucks. Just as important General George Brown, the newly appointed Seventh Air Force commander, agreed in mid-August to continue the air operations as long as needed for Vang Pao to achieve his ground objectives.

The much-delayed ground attack kicked off on August 15, 1969 with the government interdiction forces moving toward the Route 7 chokepoints in the Nong Pet area. By August 19 the southern element from San Tiau reached the base of Phou Nok Kok Mountain where they encountered some resistance, but heavy air strikes by RLAF T-28s forced the defenders to flee and Hmong guerrillas secured the position a few days later. At the same time other guerrilla fighters from Bouam Long reached LS 115 overlooking the road unopposed. Much to their surprise these forces learned from local villagers that

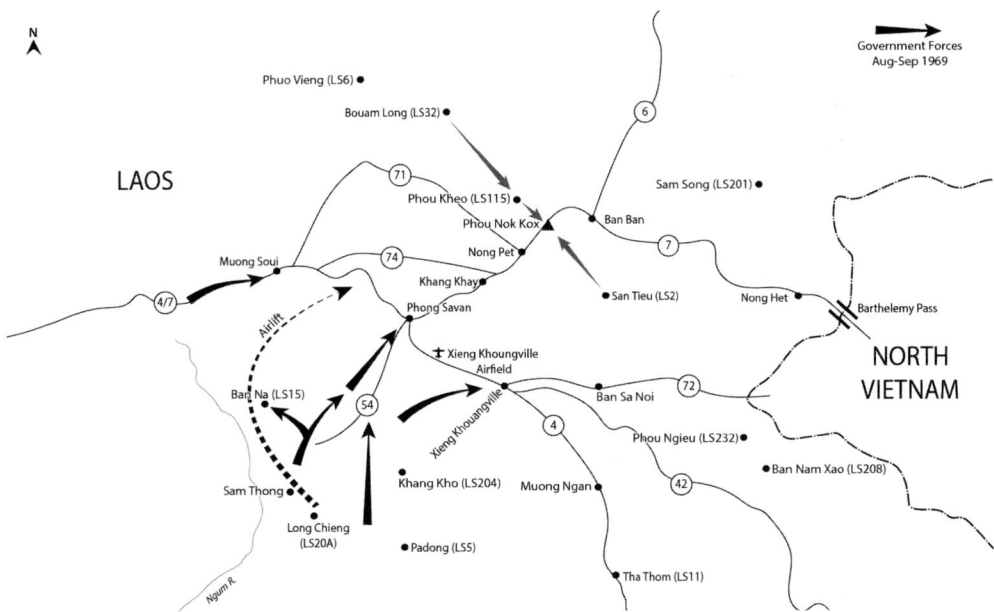

Operation About Face.

all traffic along Route 7 had been halted since the end of July. The constant air attacks, road cuts, and heavy rains had forced the communist to give up trying to move supplies through the area. Route 7 west of Ban Ban was closed for business.

The day before, on August 20, almost 3,000 men—six Hmong and three FAR battalions—began their advance toward the Plain of Jars. At the same time another combined Hmong–Neutralist force of about 800 men moved toward Muong Soui to harass the garrison there. Initially the advance by Vang Pao's main force was slowed by enemy delaying tactics, but after the first week all communist resistance suddenly and unexpectedly collapsed. In the Muong Soui area, the enemy continued to put up resistance, but quickly fell back toward the town by September.

Facing little to no opposition, both Vang Pao and the Embassy sought to exploit the battlefield situation by expanding the ground operation to now include the retaking of Muong Soui and the occupation of the Plain of Jars. The latter goal was to force the enemy into the hills to east of the plain and thus close off the supply lines running westward as long as possible before the enemy had time to regroup and counterattack. In the meantime, the communist-held towns on the westward edge of the plain, including Muong Soui, would be cut off and isolated. An American FAC described the Hmong advance as "a fantastic sight—three thousand men walking upright across the Plain of Jars"[21] who encountered only scattered resistance.

The reason soon became apparent. The bombing campaign had so completely disrupted the enemy's overextended supply lines that entire units had run out of ammunition, fuel, and food. According to a captured North Vietnamese officer, his entire 400-man unit with six tanks had only 40 rounds of ammunition and 50 gallons of fuel when Vang Pao's forces attacked.[22] Similarly another prisoner reported that his unit had received no fresh food or medical supplies since August 18. Vang Pao heaped praise on the Seventh Air Force strikes "that overwhelmed the enemy and forced him to flee in terror."[23]

It was now a mad rush for communist forces to break out to the east or take refuge in the hills before becoming completely cut off. Whole units simply disintegrated. Tanks and other heavy equipment were abandoned were they stood. Phong Savan and Khang Khay fell on September 9 following token resistance and three days later government troops walked into Xieng Khouangville unopposed. On the 20th the North Vietnamese abandoned Muong Soui, which Neutralist troops reoccupied a few days later. Across the plain a vast treasure trove of supplies and equipment that the enemy could not distribute because of the destruction of the road and logistics network was seized by Vang Pao's men, including an estimated 5 million rounds of ammunition, 6,000 weapons, 25 PT-76 tanks, 113 vehicles, 300 tons of medical supplies, and 200,000 gallons of fuel: enough to support communist forces for six months and worth some $12 million, according to CIA estimates.[24]

Throughout the remainder of September and October government forces continued to nip at the retreating enemy's heels with American and Lao planes flying more than 6,100 sorties.[25] Despite their great success, government forces suffered only light casualties in their six weeks of fighting. Exact casualty figures for the communist forces are unknown, but they were almost certainly high as many died of starvation, exposure or disease in the mountains as they attempted to flee. Others fell victim to irregular guerrilla bands or at the hands of local tribesmen and at one point Vang Paos directed 155-mm guns to rain shrapnel down on fleeing enemy. It was a bloodbath. Many units simply ceased to exist. In one battalion of the 316th Division only three survivors made it back to their lines and it would be another year before a reconstituted 316th Division returned to northern Laos.[26]

Once again disaster had been averted in the nick of time.

Loading an SA-01 acoustic sensor. (Photo Museum of the U.S. Air Force)

Operation About Face, or Operation Restore Honor as it was known in Lao, had been an unqualified success by any measure and for the first time in the war government forces were now in complete control of the Plain of Jars. Vang Pao and his men were riding high, but their euphoria wouldn't last as dark clouds were looming on the horizon. By November 1969 as the ground began to dry out, truck sightings in northeastern Laos between the North Vietnamese border and Ban Ban more than doubled and there were reports of 12,000 North Vietnamese troops massing at the border near Nong Het.[27] Seven airdropped sensor fields were established to track the buildup and the Seventh Air Force modified its interdiction approach by hitting more widely dispersed road junctions and chokepoints to complicate repair and bypass efforts. By the end of the year at least 320 trucks had been destroyed or damaged and nearly 300 road cuts made.[28] Nonetheless, this only made a dent and was at best a delaying action.

As the American concentrated on Barrel Roll interdiction efforts, the RLAF T-28s concentrated on providing close air support to the ground troops, flying more than 4,600 sorties in the last two months of the year. This was a remarkable feat in that the RLAF only averaged having 28 planes available per day. RLAF losses were also high too: 12 lost and eight heavily damaged since August.[29]

Air War in the Panhandle

Just as the U.S. interdiction campaign in southern Laos appeared to making some headway at the start of 1968, all hell broke loose as the war in South Vietnam took a dramatic turn. Accordingly, the first three months of the year would require the total commitment of every available American air asset in Southeast Asia to avoid military disaster. In early January, U.S. Marines at Khe Sanh, only about 5 miles for the Laotian border and just south of the DMZ, found themselves surrounded by an estimated 20,000 NVA troops equipped with long-range howitzers, antiaircraft artillery, and even PT-76 light tanks.

The Battle For Laos: Vietnam's Proxy War 1955-1975

North Vietnamese truck drivers receive final orders before heading into the southern Laos war zone.

Despite deep concern that Khe Sanh could become another Dien Bein Phu debacle, General Westmoreland and his commanders chose to make a stand there, believing that the overwhelming American artillery advantage and vast reserves of air power would be able to blunt any enemy attack.[30]

The battle was joined on January 21 with a sapper attack on one of Khe Sanh's external outposts that was then followed by an intense and regular artillery and mortar barrages against the main base. The siege was on and the garrison completely cutoff. As challenging as the situation was, General Momyer viewed the large enemy troop concentrations around Khe Sanh as a golden opportunity to unleash the full fury of American air power. An average day would see 350 tactical fighter strikes, 60 B-52 Arc Light sorties, and dozens of orbiting FAC aircraft directing artillery fire. Ground stations guided radar bombing missions during bad weather and precision Arc Light strikes allowed B-52s to drop their devastating payloads within three-quarters of a mile of the base's perimeter. "The tonnage of ordnance that has been placed in a five-mile circle around [the base] is unbelievable," said one Air Force commander. "It is just a landscape of splinters and bomb craters."[31]

The opening round of the battle of Khe Sanh, however, was quickly overshadowed by a much larger and grave countrywide threat—the Tet Offensive. On January 31 some 70,000 to 100,000 Viet Cong guerrillas and North Vietnamese soldiers launched an effort to capture all 36 South Vietnamese provincial capitals and Saigon in one fell swoop and thus provoke a popular uprising. These efforts were accompanied by several high-profile sapper attacks on symbols of American power, including the U.S. Embassy in Saigon and the main air bases at Bien Hoa, Tan Son Nhut, and Da Nang. Following the initial chaos, American and South Vietnamese troops with extensive close air support began to systematically expel the attackers in the coming weeks from the towns and cities they had captured. With the last of the resistance quelled by the beginning of March more than 40,000 communist fighters were dead, while the combined American and South Vietnamese losses totaled 3,400.[32]

Later that month North Vietnamese troops also began withdrawing its forces from around Khe Sanh as elements of the Army's 1st Cavalry Division linked up with the Marine defenders, lifting the 77-day siege on April 6. During the siege American planes dropped in excess of 100,000 tons of ordnance, delivered 12,400 tons of supplies, and flew nearly 25,000 sorties; they were also largely responsible for inflicting most of the estimated 10,000 to 15,000 enemy casualties.³³

Although the North Vietnamese and their Viet Cong allies had been dealt a crushing defeat on the battlefield, the ability of Hanoi to mount such a large-scale offensive in the face of the widespread U.S. bombing of North Vietnam and Laotian panhandle was particularly worrisome for Washington and Saigon. Even more disturbing was the realization that Hanoi was willing to sustain the war in the South indefinitely, a war of attrition Washington could not now afford to fight following the severe political blowback from the Tet Offensive in the United States.

By 1968 the North Vietnamese had constructed more than 2,000 thousand miles of roads crisscrossing the Laotian panhandle in an effort to circumvent U.S. interdiction efforts. (Photo Museum of the U.S. Air Force)

Still, U.S. field commanders responsible for the Steel Tiger interdiction effort in southern Laos were far from ready to throw in the towel. They firmly believed that with an intensification of current operations, the introduction of new technology and equipment, and the fine-tuning of tactics and operational procedures, significant progress could be made. And as chance would have it, several important changes were in the offing toward the end of 1968 that would have a direct and powerful bearing on future of the American air campaign in southern Laos.

First, President Johnson, in an attempt to entice the North Vietnamese back to the negotiating table and move toward a peaceful resolution to the war, ordered an end to all bombing of the North, effective November 1, 1968. The Rolling Thunder air campaign was over. This had the immediate result of freeing up large numbers of Air Force, Navy, and Marine aircraft for Laotian operations, which then saw interdiction sorties rise by 300 percent to 12,800 by the end of November.³⁴ Second, the Air Force's sensor and monitoring network—now known as Igloo White—was beginning to come into its own as the technology and support structure vastly improved. Hundreds, and soon thousands, of airdropped acoustic and seismic sensors lined various segments of the Ho Chi Minh Trail. The collected information was then relayed to airborne EC-121 aircraft and on to the Infiltration Surveillance Center at Nakhon Phanom for computer analysis. Once analyzed, targeting data could then be passed to strike aircraft for often immediate action. Likewise, the accelerated development of fixed-wing gunship armament and technology would prove to be a game-changer for the "war on trucks" that was to dominate the next several years of interdiction operations. Finally, November also saw the ending of Operation Steel Tiger and its replacement with a more refined seasonal and operational approach to targeting priority based on a rolling series of air campaigns, known as Operation Commando Hunt.

All these factors helped to serve up success for the initial dry (Commando Hunt I) and rainy (Commando Hunt II) season campaigns that ran from mid-November 1968 to mid-October 1969. Major chokepoints, such as the Mu Gai and Ban Karai passes, and key road junctions on the western side of the panhandle were heavily targeted by B-52 strikes. Meanwhile, Air Force F-4s used laser-guided bombs to create a series of "blocking belt" road cuts that were later seeded by Navy jets dropping anti-personnel mines to complicate enemy road repair efforts. In addition, Navy A-6 and A-7 aircraft dropped thousands of Mk 36 500-pound magnetic mines between these road cuts to further impede vehicle traffic.

Hidden enemy truck park near Mu Gia Pass under attack by Air Force planes. (Photo Museum of the Air Force)

These fixed-point targeting efforts were complemented by near-continuous day and night armed reconnaissance flights seeking out targets of opportunity that were located by Igloo White sensors or by roving FACs. Without a doubt, however, the best interdiction tool available for Commando Hunt operations were the Air Force's fixed-winged gunships—the AC-130A and the AC-119G—that had just recently become available. Although both planes were a considerable improvement over the old AC-47s, the AC-130 models with their 7.62-mm mini-guns, 20-mm Vulcan-Gatling guns, and 40-mm Bofors cannons, as well as an advanced array of sensors, were the most deadly. Flying out of Ubon beginning in late 1968 with the 16th Special Operations Squadron (SOS), they quickly proved especially effective at locating and destroying enemy trucks on the road at night. By October 1969 they would account for around a third of the estimated 6,000 trucks destroyed and damaged, despite flying only a fraction of the nearly 20,000 tactical Commando Hunt sorties.[35]

The North Vietnamese, however, were not standing idly by during this air assault and were constantly adapting to the changing American tactics. Dedicated repair teams were permanently positioned along heavily bombed road segments and key chokepoints. Sapper teams were formed to defuse and neutralize U.S. mines. Bypass routes were under constant construction and greater use was made of region's rivers to move supplies. Even simple diversionary tactics, like driving herds of animals along roadways, were employed to confuse American electronic sensors. The biggest countermeasure, however, was the steady increase in the number of 23-mm and 37-mm antiaircraft weapons being moved into southern Laos; by the end of 1969 almost 450 antiaircraft sites would be identified.[36] Although not nearly as dangerous a threat environment as that over North Vietnam,

Escalation

Under Vietnamization responsibility for combat operations and the defense of South Vietnam would pass from American to Vietnamese hands by 1973.

enemy antiaircraft fire would account for the loss of 68 American aircraft and the deaths of 63 pilots and crew in the first year of Commando Hunt operations.[37]

Even as the new campaign gained increasing momentum and more resources, serious questions lingered as to its effectiveness. Glowing reports of trucks destroyed or damaged, chokepoints established, road segments mined, and the destruction of large numbers of bridges, transshipment points, and storage depots by the Seventh Air Force and MACV were often met with skepticism by the CIA, State Department, and Office of the Secretary of Defense. While one side saw the interdiction effort imposing "definite, though hard to define, limits on enemy activity in South Vietnam," the other side saw the disruption as simply "not severe enough to prevent a significant increase in the rate of infiltration."[38] The effectiveness debate would continue to simmer throughout the life of Commando Hunt operations, but ultimately the interdiction effort would continue for overriding political reasons rather than purely military ones.

Honoring a pledge to deescalate the war in Vietnam and the withdrawal of U.S. forces, the newly elected administration of President Richard Nixon embarked on a policy of Vietnamization—whereby responsibility for combat operations and the defense of South Vietnam would pass from American to Vietnamese hands—in June 1969 by announcing the first troop withdrawals. Thus, the interdiction effort in southern Laos, imperfect though it was in slowing the flow of men and matériel into the South, was able to buy time for Vietnamization to take hold and provide cover for the drawdown of U.S. forces. Thus, once again the battle for Laos would be subsumed by greater geostrategic factors concerning the way forward for resolving the conflict in neighboring Vietnam, rather than in seeking a Laotian solution.

6. THE BEGINNING OF THE END

The period from 1970 to the spring of 1972 would witness many highs and lows for both sides as each sought to gain a decisive edge before the now inevitable withdrawal of American forces from Southeast Asia. Vang Pao's Hmong army would continue to bear the brunt of the fighting even as it became a shadow of its former self, while U.S. efforts to revamp the Laotian military into an effective fighting force slowly gained momentum. Meanwhile, the North Vietnamese abandoned any façade of a supporting role by outward assuming nearly all of the responsibility for combat operations. The Americans for their part were faced with twin challenges of fighting a war in the face of increasingly strident calls at home for complete military disengagement and the need to buy time so their Lao and Vietnamese allies could stand on their own once the Americans were gone. But in the meantime, both allies would rely on U.S. support more than ever just to survive.

Hanoi Strikes Back

While Operation About Face had been an overwhelming success that buoyed Hmong morale and gave the Souvanna government control over the Plain of Jars for the first time in the war, there was little realistic hope of holding on to their gains. The task was simply impossible. Arrayed against 5,500 government troops spread across the plain were at least 16,000 North Vietnamese and 6,000 Pathet Lao combat troops preparing to go on the offensive in December 1969.[1] Nonetheless, Vang Pao was unwilling to give up his hard-won gains without a fight and Souvanna further expressed his and King Savang's desire to hold onto the plain as a way to gain leverage in talks with the Pathet Lao. The communists, however, were in no mood to talk. They were spoiling for a fight—having amassed two full infantry divisions, an artillery regiment, a tank company, and six sapper and engineering battalions of North Vietnamese troops along with ten Pathet Lao battalions—and ready to inflict a serious defeat on the government forces.[2] Thus, the Americans and Vang Pao hatched a plan for a fighting withdrawal, one designed to delay the enemy advance and expose it to continuous air strikes.

The key to this delaying action was the blocking position at Phou Nok Kok overlooking Route 7. Not only did it serve to block communist supply to the west, but it anchored the northern part of the government defensive line and was held by some 600 Hmong troops. Not surprisingly, the North Vietnamese launched a four-day assault on the mountain on December 2, which failed. They tried again on the 18th, but once more were forced to retreat following stiff resistance and heavy bombing and strafing by RLAF AC-47 gunships that littered the battlefield with hundreds of mangled bodies. Unfortunately for the defenders, deteriorating weather in early January greatly limited further air support and a week-long artillery bombardment allowed yet another ground assault on January 10 to successfully capture the summit. It was a significant, but costly victory for the communist forces. During the six-week battle more than 600 North Vietnamese were believed killed and more than double that likely wounded; government forces suffered only 12 dead.³

It also should have been a major vindication of the defensive strategy, but as many American advisers feared, fighting a series of delaying actions from fixed positions would prove difficult. "We mistakenly thought we could teach them [the Hmong] defensive tactics overnight. But the idea of a phase withdrawal was alien to them."⁴ Vang Pao's troops were simply not trained or equipped for this type of conventional warfare. Thus, following the loss of Phou Nok Kok the Hmong began unilaterally abandoning their defensive positions and retreating off the plain.

President Richard Nixon and his military advisers saw ongoing Lao interdiction efforts as essential in buying time for Vietnamization to take hold. (Photo White House)

To stem this dry-season offensive, known as Campaign 319, the Seventh Air Force and RLAF did the best it could to delay the 6,000 advancing troops, flying an average of 320 sorties a day by mid-February. But poor weather and lack of visual observation forced bombing of "target areas" with marginal results and had General Brown complaining that the results were "nowhere commensurate with the effort [expended]."⁵ To address the deteriorating situation and boost Lao morale, Ambassador Goldley called upon the Joint Chiefs to support Souvanna's formal request for using B-52 heavy bombers in central Laos for the first time. Although MACV questioned the utility and lack of suitable targets for the B-52s, it agreed to a 36-plane strike against the suspected headquarters and staging area of the 312th Division. On the night of February 17/18 the U-Tapao-based bombers dropped their payloads on the headquarters complex, producing 130 huge secondary explosions that apparently destroyed numerous bunkers, but produced few casualties.

Still the communist advance continued. As an American aid worker at Sam Thong (the main refugee camp and center of Hmong civil administration) lamented, "The enemy hit us hard ... lost many positions and many men. PDJ is mostly gone. It is getting tight, morale has dropped. All women and kids, 80 percent of the people here sleep in the jungle. Worried to death where do we go from here."⁶ On February 20 a North Vietnamese battalion spearheaded by sappers and supported by PT-76 tanks attacked the airstrip at Xieng Khouangville and routed the mixed garrison of FAR, Neutralist, and Hmong troops.⁷ In a few days the last government outpost on the Plain of Jars was abandoned. Likewise, Xieng Khouangville fell on the 25th. Muong Soui was retaken by the North Vietnamese without firing a shot at the end of the month as the Neutralist defenders fled. All the territory that Vang Pao had gained the previous year was now lost and the communists were in position to assault the Hmong heartland. Many clan elders were in

The North Vietnamese began deploying large 122-mm howitzers and 130-mm towed artillery into Laos for the first time in 1971. (Photo Museum of the U.S. Air Force)

revolt, denouncing Vang Pao for destroying the Hmong people. His army was on the verge of falling completely apart. Vang Pao was despondent.[8]

The breakneck pace of the offensive, however, was beginning to take its toll on the communists. Supply lines were stretched and subject to intense American bombing, making resupply difficult. Troops were exhausted from the fighting and units needed to regroup after suffering serious casualties, estimated at between 3,500 and 6,000 since the start of the year. Time was also needed to move heavy artillery and significant ammunition stocks forward before for the final assault on the Hmong heartland. This respite allowed Vang Pao to rally his depleted forces and prepare his defenses along a line of hills just south of the plain and north of his main headquarters and the CIA's operating base at Long Chieng. Some 1,500 men were entrenched along this line with another 1,000 split between Long Chieng and Lima Site 20 at Sam Thong in the neighboring valley. He was outnumbered six to one and even with massive close air support the prospects for survival looked bleak.

The fighting resumed on March 12 with the North Vietnamese striking Vang Pao's defensive line. By the 17th the enemy had reached Skyline Ridge overlooking the Hmong headquarters and the "smell of defeat [was] in the air," according to the CIA's chief of station.[9] The main blow came against Sam Thong the next day, which quickly fell. The Seventh Air Force increased its sortie rate to 200 per day, but weather hampered their effectiveness as troops from the 316th Division moved into position. Panic began to set in among the Americans that Long Chieng could not hold without immediate reinforcements and its loss would signal the end of the Hmong army as a fighting force.

Four AC-119 gunships from Udorn were dispatched to join with Lao AC-47s providing all-night defensive fire. This proved enough to keep the enemy at bay for several days, even as the North Vietnamese worked to move their heavy artillery into position. In the meantime, Vang Pao's plea for reinforcements had been heard and FAR reinforcements from the south, as well as a 700-man "volunteer" Thai regimental combat team with three howitzers were rushed to Long Chieng. A break in the weather also allowed American, Lao, and Thai aircraft to hammer the communist positions as well as their exposed supply lines. By March 26, Vang Pao had been reinforced to 3,400 men and he counterattacked under an air umbrella to recapture lost positions on Skyline Ridge.[10] A separate force was sent to retake Sam Thong, which was recovered on the 30th.

The Beginning of the End

Although they fought bravely, the lightly armed defenders of Ban Na (LS 15) were no match against the better-equipped and veteran North Vietnamese troops.

Over the coming weeks, government forces and their Thai volunteers pressed the attack as the communist troops fell back toward the plain. At the same time the Seventh Air Force pummeled key interdiction points on Route 7, flying 844 sorties between April and June and effectively closing down this supply line.[11] Before departing, however, the North Vietnamese launched another fierce attack in May on Bouam Long (now known as "the Fortress" of the lima site crescent) on the northern edge of the plain. They were rebuffed again, suffering heavy losses once again at the hands of Moua Cher Pao's men and LS 32 remained in government hands and a continuing thorn in the side of the communists on the plain. By early summer Vang Pao had likewise reoccupied his defensive line just south of the plain as the rains came in earnest. Once again disaster had been averted at the last moment.

After a brief respite and as the Air Force continued its Barrel Roll interdiction efforts, Vang Pao undertook a limited rainy-season offensive, Operation Counterpunch, in August. Poor visibility limited air support and stubborn enemy resistance slowed the advance through September, but improving weather and strong support from the RLAF—2,400 sorties in October alone—allowed the offensive to gain momentum.[12] Running low on supplies and ammunition thanks to the American interdiction effort, the enemy fell back toward Route 4 on the center of the plain. Muong Soui was recaptured on October 11, Ban Na to the south fell a few weeks later, and Phou Seu overlooking Route 4 was occupied at the end of October. Content with these modest gains in pushing the enemy away from his base, Vang Pao moved to consolidate his position and await the communists' next move.

Despite his improved tactical position, Vang Pao's long-term prospects were poor. The CIA noted that his forces "had never been stretched thinner or seem quite as close to the

CIA paramilitary adviser with Hmong officers near Long Chieng.

breaking point. Nor had they ever before been forced to rely as much on outside help [for their survival]."¹³ The Embassy assessment was just as bleak, reporting that if the Hmong were to suffer severe losses that year, "it would be difficult, if not impossible for Vang Pao to prevent his troops from joining their dependents in a mass exodus."¹⁴

Times They Are a Changing

The new decade of the 1970s ushered in several important political and military developments outside of Laos that would have a significant impact on the course of war.

Since May 1968, American and North Vietnamese officials had been engaged in on-again-off-again talks aimed at negotiating an end to the war even as each side sought to gain the upper hand on the battlefield. The situation in Laos was clearly a side issue, but one Hanoi sought to turn to its political advantage especially in the wake of public revelations of American involvement there following the February B-52 strikes. Nixon's public acknowledgement of American military engagement in Laos in March 1970 after more than a decade of U.S. denials, not only further fueled antiwar sentiment in Congress and calls for greater restrictions, but it gave Hanoi diplomatic cover for increasing its aggression. Not surprisingly, North Vietnamese negotiators rebuffed American proposals to mutually deescalate military operations. Hanoi knew it had a winning hand in Laos and it was going to play it out.

Any doubts about the Nixon administration's commitment to its policy of Vietnamization and disengagement were also clearly being dispelled. From a peak of nearly 550,000 men in April 1969, American troop levels would fall to 334,000 by the end of 1970 and be on pace to fall by half again within another year.¹⁵ Under Secretary of Defense Melvin Laird's direction the United States was working to equip, train, and create a South Vietnamese military that would be capable of assuming full responsibility for the security of South Vietnam by 1973. In the meantime, critical logistics and combat support functions—most notably air and fire support missions—would remain largely in American hands and Washington warned that any escalating North Vietnamese aggression would jeopardize American troop withdrawals and elicit "strong and effective [military] measures" in response.[16] By shifting the burden of the fighting to the South Vietnamese, the Nixon administration sought to buy time for itself to reach an acceptable peace agreement with Hanoi while limiting U.S. casualties and thus undercutting the antiwar movement's calls for a quick unilateral withdrawal of all American troops. Nothing was said of Laos, but clearly the Americans were planning on leaving Southeast Asia and the meant from Laos too.

Even though the administration was bent on drawing down American forces, it still needed to project an image of strength and resolve, to deter Hanoi from exploiting the changing battlefield balance and also to reassure Saigon of America's continuing commitment to its defense. The opportunity arose in April 1970 when Nixon ordered a joint U.S.–South Vietnamese cross-border strike into Cambodia to shore up the newly installed anti-communist government of Lon Nol. On April 30 American and South Vietnamese forces numbering nearly 25,000 troops crossed the border into Cambodia to drive an estimated 40,000 North Vietnamese and Viet Cong from their sanctuaries, destroy their supplies, and disrupt their operations. The president defended his decision to the American people as necessary to protect U.S. troops still in Vietnam and to guarantee the continued success of the withdrawal and of Vietnamization. Nonetheless, the invasion sparked massive antiwar protest in the United States and led to Congress passing legislation "prohibiting any U.S. forces from operating on [the] ground inside Cambodia or Laos."[17] Any glimmer of hope of having American troops coming to the aid of the Lao government was permanently dashed. Moreover, the CIA dejectedly concluded that the 67,000 North Vietnamese troops now in Laos had the "last word on priorities" and Hanoi was clearly the one calling the shots.[18]

These congressional restrictions on military operations in Southeast Asia and the accompanying cutting in war funding soon had a profound impact on the war in Laos. The summer of 1970 saw the deactivation of the 11th Tactical Reconnaissance Squadron at Udorn, a cut by two-thirds in the number of A-1s with the 56th SOW at Nakhon Phanom, and the return of 60 F-105 fighters to the United States.[19] Likewise, the size of the Seventh Air Force staff was cut by half, which eliminated the tactical control center responsible for planning and monitoring Barrel Roll operations. The greatest impact, however, would come in the form of a congressionally mandated ceiling of 10,000 sorties per month for all of Southeast Asia, which forced U.S. commanders to make increasingly difficult choices. The emphasis on interdiction to counter any potential North Vietnamese buildup in the South meant that Commando Hunt operations would receive roughly 70 percent of the monthly allocations, with the remaining 30 percent divided equally among Barrel Roll, South Vietnam, and Cambodia sorties.[20]

Thus, from a peak of just over 200 Barrel Roll sorties per day during the 1968–70 period, the Air Force would now be limited to less than 35 per day. It was expected that the RLAF would pick up much of the slack. But with just 35 T-28s operational by October and those planes carrying much smaller payloads than Air Force F-4s and A-1s, the ability of air

Fly Until You Die: The Story of the Hmong Pilots

Air power, and in particular close air support, proved often to be a decisive factor in many of the campaigns and battles fought out across northern Laos. While the bulk of this effort came from the Americans, the fledging Royal Lao Air Force (RLAF) grew over time to become a significant player in the air order of battle. The development of which was made possible by the U.S. military training program known as Project Water Pump based out of the Thai air base at Udorn since early 1964. Much less, however, is known of the special squadron of fearless Hmong pilots that operated directly under the command of General Vang Pao from his base at Long Chieng.

The first two Hmong pilots—including the soon-to-be legendary, Lue Lee—graduated from Water Pump training and pinned on their wings in January 1968; by 1974 a total of 37 Hmong officers had successfully completed the pilot training. Although a few were also qualified to fly helicopters and C-47s, their plane of choice was the T-28D attack aircraft. The planes were the perfect choice—easy to fly with powerful engines, strengthened wing hard points for carrying 1,200-pound ordnance loads, and very durable. However, the quality of individual aircraft varied, as the T-28s were constantly adapted and stitched together to keep them flying.

As a group all T-28 pilots in Laos used the call sign *Chao Pha Khao*, which translates as "master of the white mountains," but the Hmong pilots were considered the bravest of the brave. One former pilot recalled, "The biggest fear is when you are approaching the target [and] did not know from which direction the antiaircraft [fire] would come. But at the moment when you drop your bombs and hear explosions, you just let go. My plane was hit many times ... but they were just small guns, like AK, so not too bad." They became Vang Pao's "flying artillery" and he pushed them to the limit when times were most desperate in fending off massed North Vietnamese infantry assaults or when a position needed to be captured at all cost. On days when Vang Pao directed the bombing, as he often did, "when you accurately hit a target, he just said good, and that's it, [but] when you missed a target, he cursed excessively as if he wanted you dead," remembers one pilot. Whether it was dropping 250-pound bombs on enemy positions or staffing with their .50-caliber guns the pilots responded and their mere presence often was enough to raise the morale of Hmong troops on the ground. Many pilots often flew eight to ten sorties a day, easily surpassing the 100 sorties-per-month mark—which equaled the number of sorties a U.S. Air Force pilot would fly in an entire year in Southeast Asia.

Though even the best of the best, like Ly Lue, were not immortal and his death in July 1969 while attacking an enemy gun position at Muong Soui devastated his fellow pilots and left Vang Pao overwhelmed by grief. Crowds came to honor him during his three-day funeral at Long Chieng that was attended by American and Lao dignitaries. While Ly Lue's dead demoralized some pilots, others became even more determined to finish the fight he had started. It would end up costing many of their lives too; 17 or nearly half of all the Hmong pilots would be dead by war's end.

(Sources: C. Vang, *Fly Until You Die*; J. Hamilton-Merritt, *Tragic Mountains*, pp. 189-215)

power to alter the military balance was now in question. This was new reality facing the Souvanna government and General Vang Pao as a new year dawned.

Teetering on the Edge

As he anxiously awaited the communist dry-season 1970/1 offensive to begin in earnest, Vang Pao had much to worry about beyond the declining levels of American air support and whether his cobbled together force of Hmong and other highland tribesmen, Thai volunteers, and handful of FAR troops would be able to slow the enemy advance on Long Chieng. Not only was his army a hollow shell of its former self, but his people were teetering on the brink of extinction. The battle for Laos had become a war of survival for the Hmong. So many men, women, and children had died, close to 30,000 now or 12 percent of the Hmong population. Teenage company commanders were leading troops who were little more than children. Inexperienced soldiers also meant more battlefield deaths, forcing Vang Pao to dig even deeper into the ranks of young boys and old men and the loss of so many young men made it increasingly difficult for young women to find husbands, further undermining the society.[21] Still he knew he had to fight on, he had little choice.

The communist offensive finally got underway in January 1971 with about 6,000 NVA troops bypassing Vang Pao's defensive line south of Route 4 to seize Muong Soui in early February before turning toward Long Chieng, about 30 miles to the south. Several lima sites atop the mountainous terrain—notably Ban Na (LS 15)—barred the enemy advance and were soon surrounded and had to be resupplied by air. Hmong and RLAF T-28 sorties surged to 44 per day to help keep the communist attackers at bay. As the fighting continued to rage around the lima sites, other North Vietnamese infantry and artillery units continued toward Long Chieng where they began to shell the base and its defenses on Skyline Ridge during February and March. Several minor infantry probes were also mounted, but for the most part the enemy was content to pound away at the defenders with their heavy artillery.

The Air Force responded by doubling its sortie rate to 60 per day and between February 11 and March 30 flew 1,525 sorties in close air support and another 1,025 against enemy supply lines and interdiction points along the Plain of Jars.[22] Five AC-119 gunships of the 18th SOS out of Nakhon Phanom also joined with two Lao AC-47s to provide nighttime covering fire for the lima sites and the Skyline Ridge defenses. American B-52 bombers also returned to northern Laos, flying 149 sorties over the next three months against enemy supply depots with good results.[23] The North Vietnamese countered by bringing in increasing numbers of antiaircraft weapons to defend their supply lines and protect their troops from air attack. Although far less a dangerous environment than in the panhandle, North Vietnamese air defenses in northern Laos would claim eight Air Force planes and the lives of nine crewmen during 1971.[24] All this, however, was enough to stymie the communist offensive, which sputtered to a halt at the end of April with the onset of the rainy season. Long Chieng had held again.

The start of the rainy season also ushered in a dilemma for the Americans and their Lao allies. Ambassador Godley and the Seventh Air Force encouraged Vang Pao and the Souvanna government to use the time to rest and rebuild, especially given the progress on molding a new Royal Lao Army (RLA) into a reasonably effective military after years

An Air America helicopter resupplying Thai troops defending a position on the Plain of Jars.

of atrophy. Moreover, they pointed out the limited availability of American air support given recent restrictions and the prospect of having the northern Laos daily sortie rate cut in half by July. Now was not the time to go on the offensive. Not surprisingly, Vang Pao had other ideas. With the encouragement of Souvanna and King Savang, who wanted to strengthen their hands in peace talks with the Pathet Lao that were running in parallel to the U.S. talks with the North Vietnamese, Vang Pao prepared to retake the Plain of Jars in a repeat of his 1969 triumph, appropriately naming the new offensive Operation About Face II.

Following yet another successful defense of Bouam Long and LS 32 north of the plain in May, thanks to the tenacity of Moua Cher Pao's 800 men, radar-directed gunships, and tactical fighter strikes, Vang Pao's rainy-season offensive got moving much to the annoyance of the Air Force. Although the Seventh Air Force finally agreed to provide F-4s and A-1s to support the advance, the deputy commander chastised the Embassy for allowing the operation to move forward by questioning "the wisdom of a ground effort" in light of "the current policy to wind down the war and decommit air and ground forces whenever possible."25

After some initial resistance, the enemy began falling back toward the Plain of Jars in June. Although still greatly outnumbered, government troops were airlifted by Air America helicopters to surround enemy positions that were then hammered by T-28 and A-1 strikes. Several thousand enemy troops, however, continued to hold forward positions to the east of the Phou Pha Xai Mountain even as Vang Pao marched onto the plain. By mid-July his forces had captured an estimated 800 tons of supplies, destroyed or captured numerous pieces of field artillery (including one D-30 122-mm gun taken back to Long Chieng as a war trophy and installed in front of Vang Pao's house), and advanced up to Route 4.26 Here the communist defenses stiffened along a defensive arc running from Phong Savan to Xieng Khouangville as the offensive ground to a halt by September. Unable to advance and unwilling to retreat, Vang Pao's forces dug in and established a series of six mutually supporting, mountaintop firebases manned by Thai artillery units and protected by infantry detachments. Meanwhile, the Seventh Air Force began an interdiction campaign—limited though it was to less than 20 sorties per day—to slow the communist supply buildup for the inevitable dry-season counterattack.27

The blow came on December 18 with some 12,000 North Vietnamese and Pathet Lao troops launching Campaign Z, spearheaded by the 312th and the now-rebuilt 316th

The Beginning of the End

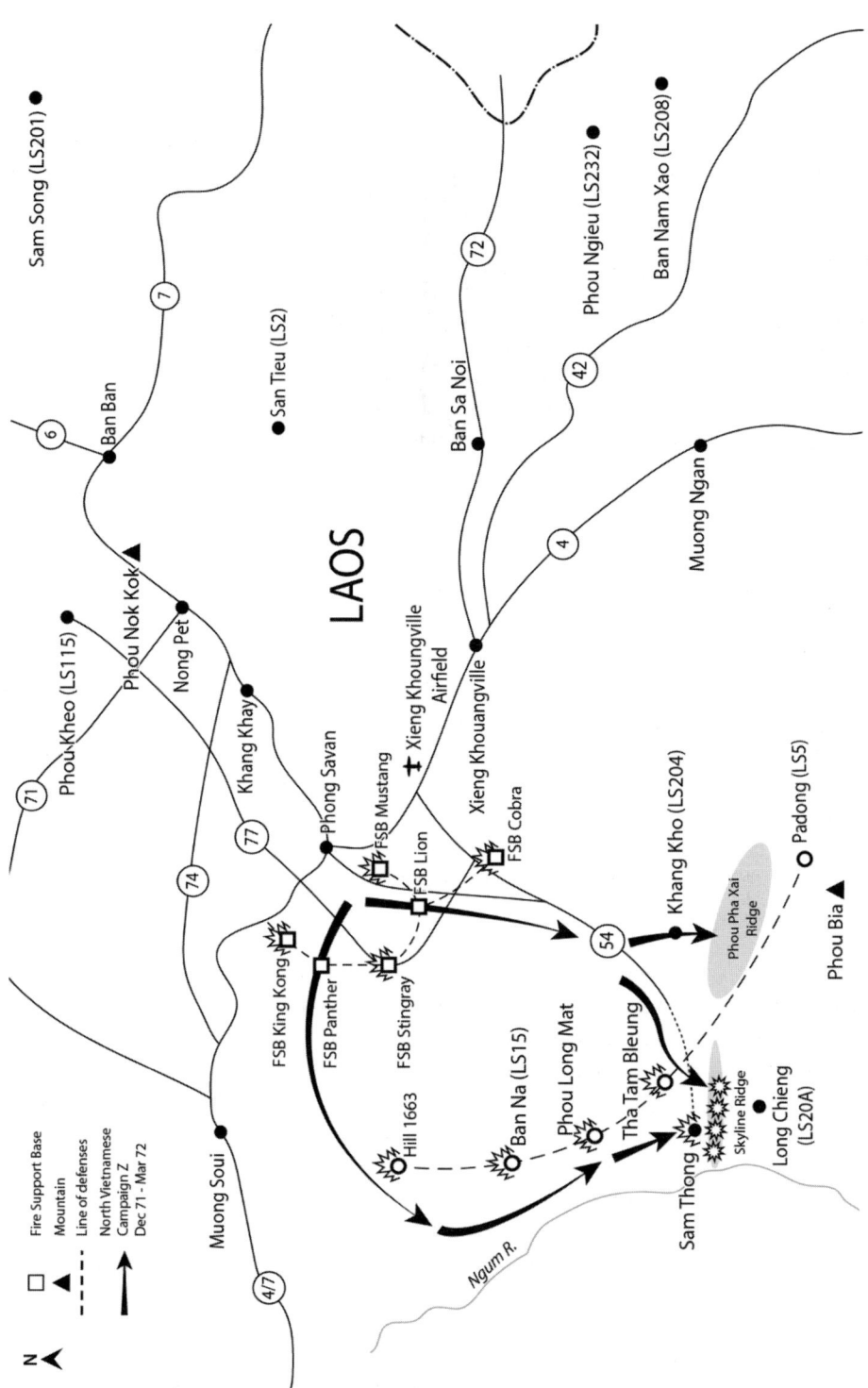

Defending the Hmong Heartland.

divisions, along with two additional infantry regiments, and six artillery and tank battalions.[28] Noteworthy too were the inclusion of long-range, Soviet-made M-46 130-mm towed field artillery guns and even T-34 medium tanks for the first time. Opposing this force were about 5,000 men that Vang Pao deployed across three consecutive defensive lines—beginning with the mini Maginot Line of firebases—between Route 4 and ending at Skyline Ridge outside Long Chieng, which the Embassy assessed would hold up with "adequate" air support.[29] The Embassy was wrong. Within 72 hours of the enemy launching their attack every one of the forward firebases was overrun after a punishing shelling that drove the defenders into their bunkers, then followed by massed infantry assaults assisted by PT-76 tank cannon fire. Shell-shocked and suffering concussion, bleeding from their ears and noses, the Thai and Hmong defenders didn't stand a chance: 286 were killed, 418 wounded, and an estimated 1,500 missing.[30]

American and Hmong aircraft scrambled to come to the rescue as frantic calls for help filled the airwaves, but it was too late. Nonetheless, the planes braved heavy antiaircraft to assist the fleeing survivors; two T-28s were shot down, along with an Air America helicopter. Arriving A-1s and F-4s quickly encountered another problem—MiG-21 fighters. Two Phantoms were downed on December 18 and a third crashed from fuel starvation following an air-to-air engagement.[31] While North Vietnamese MiGs had conducted hit-and-run attacks on American aircraft flying interdiction missions near the Lao border, this was the first instance of the fighters operating over central Laos and in conjunction with a ground offensive. The Air Force pilots would learn these hard lessons, recovering to even the score with the MiGs in the early months of 1972 by downing three without loss.[32]

In spite of the Seventh Air Force allocating 46 fighters and six gunships to the fight, the advancing North Vietnamese juggernaut—using T-34 tanks in an assault role for the first time—smashed through the weakly held lima site defensive line. Not only did the North Vietnamese tanks terrify the Hmong, but the defenders lacked any basic antitank weapons to counter them. The defensive line collapsed completely on January 11. The enemy was closing in on Long Chieng and all that stood between them were the defenses at Sam Thong and along Skyline Ridge.

The Americans scrambled to bring in all available Lao and Thai volunteer reinforcements, as well as additional artillery, but several of the RLA mobile groups were under-strength or of dubious quality. More concerning was the CIA's chief of station's belief that Vang Pao was "losing his grip" and his troops were "drifting beyond effective control."[33] While undoubtedly in one of his dark moods, it was soon discovered that the general was suffering from viral pneumonia and was quickly hospitalized. To also help stave off the enemy advance, B-52s out of U-Tapao were called in, but heavy clouds and overcast combined with the lack of precision targeting data made the moving enemy difficult to hit from 25,000 feet, much less slow him down.

In the meantime, all three regiments of the 312th Division were bearing down on Skyline Ridge and well-camouflaged 130-mm guns several valleys over began raining down high-explosive shells on the defenders and Long Chieng itself. Since the big guns far outranged the Thai 105-mm and 155-mm howitzers on hand, little could be done to silence them with counterbattery fire and even the orbiting Ravens found them almost

The Beginning of the End

Above left: Air Force personnel plotting targeting and strike activity at the Infiltration Surveillance Center at Nakhon Phanom, Thailand. (Photo Museum of the U.S. Air Force)

Above right: An O-2 "Oscar Deuce" of the 23rd Tactical Air Support Squadron prepares to leave on a forward air control mission over southern Laos in 1971. (Photo Museum of the U.S. Air Force)

impossible to spot and target. In addition, enemy sappers raided Long Chieng twice in early January, damaging a command post, an ammunition dump, and several parked FAC aircraft.

Mid-January saw some intensive fighting on the ridge as Mobile Group 30 with the aid of RLAF T-28s sought to push back an enemy incursion.[34] Throughout the next several weeks both sides continued to spar along the ridge to gain a tactical advantage with neither gaining the upper hand. It was the enemy road-building effort from the plain to Sam Thong, however, that concerned the Americans and Vang Pao the most. For once the new Route 54 was completed it would allow the North Vietnamese to bring forward more 122-mm D-30 howitzers and 130-mm towed field guns, T-34 tanks, and heavy equipment. Air strikes were hampered by poor visibility and antiaircraft fire, so the road work continued to make progress, but the AC-119s did exact a toll on enemy trucks by damaging or destroying almost 952 in three months.[35]

The seriousness of the situation provoked a heated debate among American officials. Many in Washington were worried about Long Chieng becoming "another Dien Bien Phu" and advocated for a phased fighting withdrawal to the Vientiane Plain. This, they claimed, would limit government casualties and allow air power to pound the advancing attackers and their extended supply lines. The Embassy and CIA advocated for defending the base at all cost, because abandoning it would risk forever shattering Hmong morale and destroy Vang Pao's authority. In the end, the basic realities of Laotian warfare and the situation on the ground carried the day. It was Long Chieng or nothing.

Thus, began the biggest battle of the war and the one with the greatest stakes on the line. On March 11 an opening enemy artillery barrage was followed by armor and infantry attacks on Sam Thong. The resulting fighting was especially bitter with savage hand-to-hand combat throughout the valley as tactical aircraft, gunships, and even B-52s added to

The Battle For Laos: Vietnam's Proxy War 1955–1975

 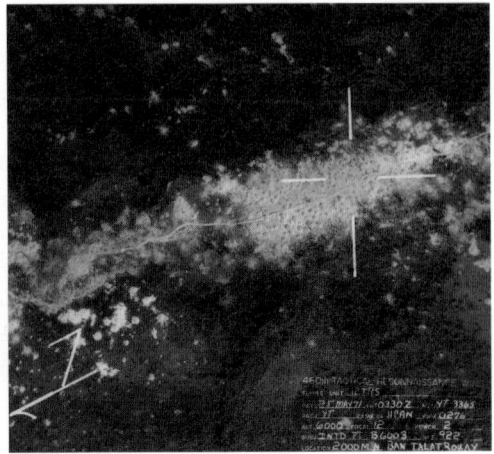

Above left: The Americans did their best to target major chokepoints, like this river crossing, with repeated bombings; note derelict bridge piers to the right. (Photo Museum of the U.S. Air Force)

Above right: Heavily cratered road segment in eastern Saravane Province near the South Vietnamese border, May 1971. (Photo Museum of the U.S. Air Force)

the carnage. Of particular note was the use of the B-52s in a close air support role, flying 318 sorties against targets in the Sam Thong–Long Chieng area.[36]

Under this pressure, the best came out in the defenders, who fought like their lives were dependent on repelling the enemy—which they were. Hmong and FAR troops hurled grenades against T-34 tanks, while Hmong pilots dove headlong into the chaos spraying enemy troops and tanks with gunfire and rockets. Thai gunners leveled their howitzers and fired point blank at the oncoming enemy and many died when their guns were overrun. It still wasn't enough and by March 18 Vang Pao was forced to pull back from the Sam Thong valley.

The momentum of the enemy assault was enough to carry the North Vietnamese infantry onto Skyline Ridge. But they could advance no farther. Suffering heavy casualties, they were a spent force. Determined counterattacks by the Thai battalions repeatedly drove the enemy back, but the meat grinder that was Skyline Ridge cost them dearly.[37] One last enemy armor thrust failed when several of the lead tanks were crippled by landmines. Over the next weeks Hmong fighters worked their way along the ridge clearing out pockets of isolated enemy troops. With the onset of April rains resupply became increasingly difficult so the North Vietnamese began pulling back to the Plain of Jars.

In an effort to block this withdrawal and trap what it could of the deadly 130-mm guns and other heavy ordnance, the Seventh Air Force launched a targeted interdiction effort to choke off Route 54. However, on March 30, Hanoi launched its Easter Offensive in South Vietnam that diverted every available American aircraft to that battlefield so the North Vietnamese were able to withdraw largely intact from Sam Thong. Cautiously nipping at the heels of the retreating enemy, Vang Pao's forces were able to push forward and reoccupy the old lima site defensive line by June.

Buying Time in the Panhandle

As the bitter contest in central Laos raged back and forth in late 1969 through the spring of 1972, the U.S. interdiction effort in the panhandle continued to grind on. In Commando Hunt operations the Americans thought they had found the answer. The combination of AC-119 and AC-130 gunships, C-123s equipped with bomblet canisters, and Igloo White sensors, was believed to be responsible for destroying or damaging thousands of enemy trucks; one estimate ranged up to 10,000 between late 1969 and 1970.[38] Combined with B-52 strikes against the mountain passes and day and night tactical sorties, American military planners believed that no more than one-third of supplies were reaching enemy forces in South Vietnam.[39] CIA analysts, however, continued to be less sanguine. Regardless of its true effectiveness, the interdiction effort was seen as critical in buying time for Vietnamization to take hold and for the American troop withdrawal to continue.

However, rising U.S. congressional opposition to the war and associated budgetary cutbacks in early 1970 reduced not only aircraft levels in Southeast Asia, but the sortie rate for Commando Hunt operations as well. The joint American–South Vietnamese cross-border incursion into Cambodia in April and May, as well as the need for extensive air support to counter the 1970/1 communist offensive in central Laos also negatively impacted the interdiction effort. Hanoi took advantage of this respite to push more men and equipment down the trail, which had American commanders believing that preparation for a major offensive in the South was in the works. Thus with American backing, Saigon launched Operation Lam Son 719 in February 1971.

Lam Son 719 was designed to strike a powerful blow against a key North Vietnamese logistics hub in southern Laos, destroy huge supply stockpiles, and thus thwart any communist pre-offensive buildup in the panhandle. U.S. congressional restrictions prohibited the use of any American ground troops in the operation and with the exception of American air support—which would be quite extensive—the South Vietnamese would be on their own. The plan called for an initial thrust on February 8 into Laos along Route 9 by roughly 6,200 troops, to be followed by an advance with mechanized and artillery support on the town of Tchepone some 25 miles from the border. Additional units would be airlifted by U.S. helicopters along the line of advance to safeguard the flanks of the column and destroy any enemy resistance. At the same time, the RLA's Mobile Group 33 would advance from the west with four battalions to cut Route 23 and then link up with South Vietnamese troops at Tchepone. American tactical aircraft, including everything from gunships to jets and B-52 bombers, would help clear the way and provide close air support to the advancing column. By the end of the operation U.S. planes would drop more than 30,000 tons of bombs in support of the operation.[40] By February 12 about 10,000 South Vietnamese were operating inside Laos.

Things began to go awry early on in the operation. The slow pace of the advance gave the enemy time to call in reinforcements from the more than five divisions that were reported to be in southern Laos at the time.[41] The armor column of tanks, armored personnel carriers, and artillery became bogged down and unable to maneuver off the confining road and river valley, presenting inviting targets for North Vietnamese artillery. After advancing only 12 miles many units began to dig in and call upon American air support to stem the increasingly aggressive attacks on the flanks. The Americans

The Battle For Laos: Vietnam's Proxy War 1955–1975

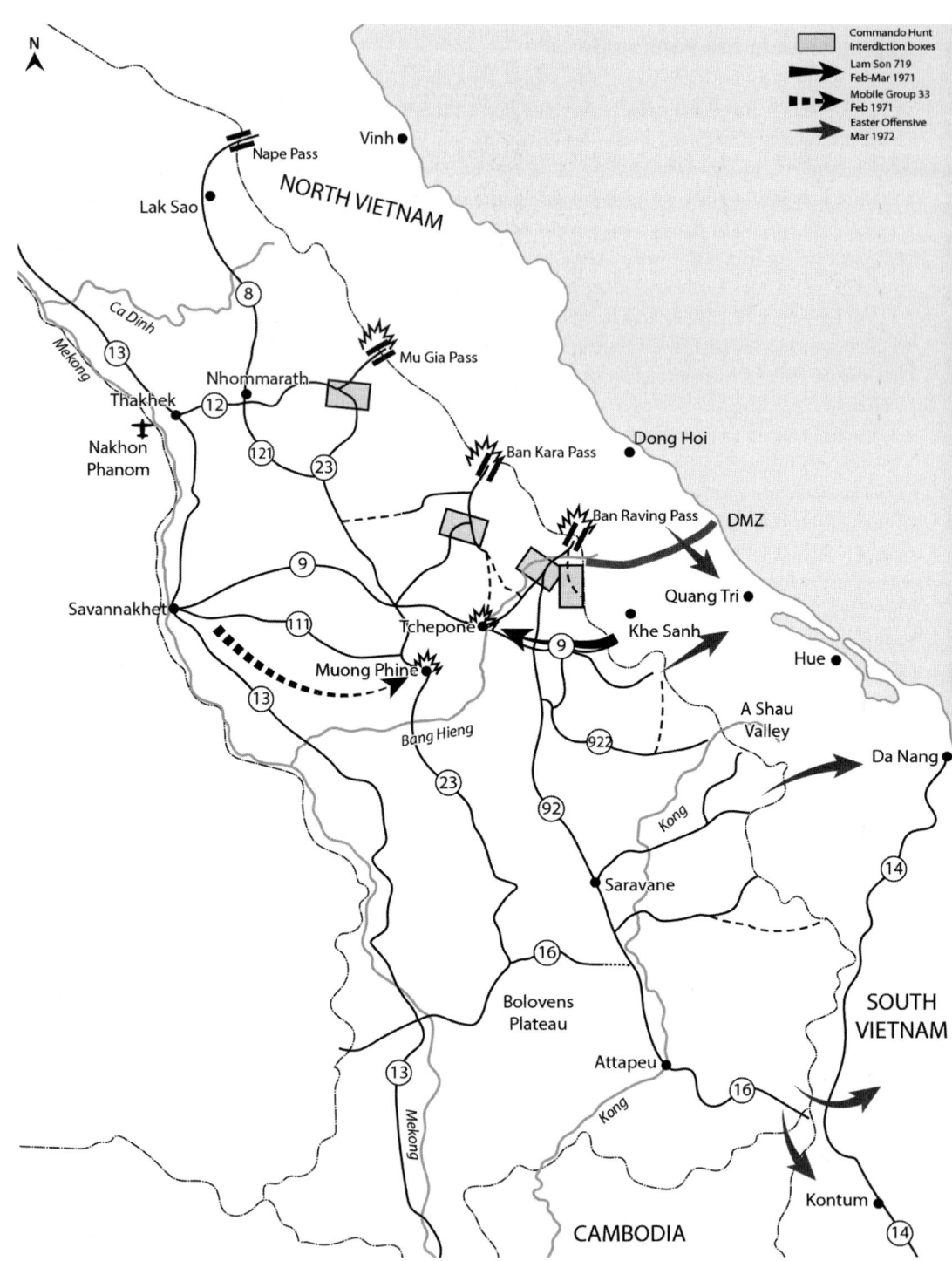

Southern Laos Area of Operations, 1971.

responded, but poor coordination and confusion on the ground hindered the effectiveness of air strikes. To the west, Mobile Group 33 was able to capture Muong Phine and came within seven miles of Tchepone on February 20, but a vicious North Vietnamese assault forced it onto the defensive. Elements of the invading South Vietnamese force did eventually reach the vacated town on March 7, destroying or capturing what the enemy couldn't remove, but now it was facing some 20,000 counterattacking North Vietnamese soldiers supported by tanks and artillery. Facing mounting casualties, Saigon ordered its troops to withdraw. To make matters worse the withdrawal quickly turned into a disorderly rout as many battle-weary units broke and fled, abandoning large amounts of weapons and other military hardware along the way, as the North Vietnamese nipped at their heels. By March 24 nearly all South Vietnamese troops were out of Laos and the operation was officially declared over on April 6.

Armored personnel carriers and tanks spearheaded the drive up Route 9 in the opening days of February 1971 as part of Operation Lam Son 719.

Both sides suffered heavy losses in men and equipment. The North Vietnamese lost an estimated 14,500 killed (about one-third from air strikes), an unknown number of wounded, about 20 tons of supplies, and had at least five dozen tanks destroyed. South Vietnamese losses were reported as 1,519 killed, 5,423 wounded, and 651 missing, along with some 75 tanks, large numbers of armored personnel carriers, and nearly 200 crew-served weapons. American fixed-wing losses were relatively light—seven aircraft—but the Army lost over 100 helicopters in the two months of fighting; American dead totaled 176.[42] While the operation did disrupt the enemy's logistics pipeline and caused considerable losses in men and matériel, Hanoi would impressively be able to quickly rebuild and make good its losses in a less than a year. Moreover, by March 1972, it would be able to launch the largest ground offensive in South Vietnam since the 1968 Tet Offensive.

Commando Hunt VII, the 1971/2 dry-season interdiction campaign, exemplified the difficult challenges facing the Americans in Laos at this stage of the war. Given a marked expansion of the road network by the North Vietnamese during the recent monsoon season, the Seventh Air Force was forced to expand the operating area beyond Steel Tiger, yet it had fewer aircraft available to work with. From a peak in 1968 the aircraft order of battle had fallen from 621 tactical jets to 226 and from 105 B-52 bombers to 54 by late 1971.[43] On the plus side, the number of AC-130 gunships had risen from six to 18 over the past year. In addition, Commando Hunt sorties were also reduced by nearly 30 percent, having

The Battle For Laos: Vietnam's Proxy War 1955-1975

Although no American troops were involved, U.S. helicopters played an essential role in airlifting South Vietnamese forces into Laos as part of Operation Lam Son 719.

to compete with other battlefield demands in northern Laos, South Vietnam, and the recently instigated "protective reaction" retaliatory strikes in the North Vietnamese panhandle north of the DMZ. There simply weren't enough aircraft to go around.

To bridge the gap new battlefield technology and upgraded armaments were introduced to improve the efficiency of Commando Hunt operations. Enhanced and improved Igloo White sensor arrays; aircraft equipped with low-light, infrared, and laser detection and targeting systems; and upgraded AC-130s with 105-mm howitzers and improved sensor arrays were introduced. Likewise the improved accuracy of radar bombing and the use of F-4 fighters equipped with laser-guided bombs increased the accuracy and kill rate of the missions. Upgrades to equipment and a revamped command and control structure at the Infiltration Surveillance Center at Nakhon Phanom also helped improve targeting and made better use of the available aircraft.

Still, air commanders and operation planners were also forced to make hard decisions in their target selection and operational strategy to make up for the shortfall in aircraft and sorties. At the start of Commando Hunt VII in November 1971, the focus was on hitting the main entry points into Laos, primarily the Mu Gia, Ban Karai, and Ban Raving passes, along with the western end of the DMZ. B-52s and laser-guided F-4s carried much of this burden. Follow-on operations in early 1972 then concentrated on establishing a series of "blocking belts" at key transportation hubs through creation of road cuts. Once again, aerial mining was used to seed the road cuts with anti-personnel mines to complicate road repairs. The next phase called for tactical aircraft and B-52s to pound seven main exit points from Laos into Cambodia and South Vietnam.

This task was further complicated by the proliferation of North Vietnamese air defense measures. From April 1971 to November 1971 the number of estimated anti-aircraft guns in the panhandle more than doubled, rising from about 700 to perhaps 1,500.[44] Moreover, many of these additional weapons were the greater-range 57-mm guns, which along with the large number of existing 12.7-mm to 37-mm weapons made defenses in the panhandle the strongest to date. Hanoi also deployed a small, but significant number of radar-controlled 85-mm and 100-mm guns by 1972 to protect key targets such as the mountain passes.

Even more threatening to American aircraft were the SA-2 surface-to-air missiles deployed near the Laotian border with the first firing on a Navy jet—and missing—near

The Beginning of the End

Above left: Wounded South Vietnamese troops being evacuated during Lam Son 719.

Above right: By the end of 1971, U.S. intelligence estimated that the North Vietnamese had deployed upward of 1,500 antiaircraft weapons in the Laotian panhandle. (Photo Museum of the U.S. Air Force)

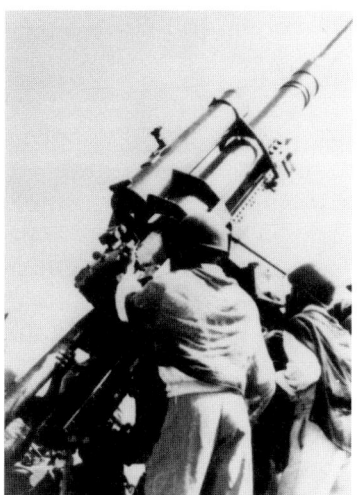 

Above left: North Vietnamese 85-mm antiaircraft guns were commonly used to defend priority targets like mountain passes. (Photo Museum of the U.S. Air Force)

Above right: The slow-moving AC-119 gunships could inflict serious damage against enemy trucks and vehicles, but they were also highly vulnerable to ground fire as this wing damage shows. (Photo Museum of the U.S. Air Force)

Mu Gia Pass on November 2. In mid-December the SAM crews scored their first kills, downing an Air Force F-105G Wild Weasel and forcing an F-4 to spin out of control and crash as it sought to avoid a missile.[45] By February 1972 more than 50 missiles had

The Battle For Laos: Vietnam's Proxy War 1955–1975

The new threat to Commando Hunt interdiction operations: SA-2 missiles. (Photo Museum of the U.S. Air Force)

SAM crews claimed their first victim over Laos when they downed an Air Force F-105G Wild Weasel that was supporting a B-52 strike near Mu Gia Pass on December 10, 1971. (Photo Museum of the U.S. Air Force)

been launched at attacking U.S. aircraft with an additional F-4D lost. Over the course of Commando Hunt VII, enemy antiaircraft fire would account for the loss of 13 U.S. aircraft, while SA-2 batteries would claim another ten.[46]

Although not as successful in chalking up victories, the regular appearance of MiG fighters over southern Laos forced the American to divert more aircraft to combat air patrol and escort operations. From November 1971 to March 1972, 76 MiG-21s and four MiG-19s made 58 separate penetrations of southern Laotian airspace.[47] And while they shot down no planes, they effectively forced the Americans to react to the incursions, often aborting or diverting strike missions.

Commando Hunt VII—and all U.S. interdiction operations in southern Laos—came to an end on March 31 with the start of the 1972 Easter Offensive that diverted all available aircraft to the South Vietnamese battlefield. By that time U.S. pilots had flown about 31,500 sorties with B-52s adding another 3,176 to the mix.[48] Some 70 percent of the tactical strikes were against interdiction points, transshipment points and storage areas, and against trucks. The North Vietnamese were estimated to have lost 10,689 trucks damaged or destroyed—more than two-thirds of this total by AC-130 gunships—and had about 85 percent of their supplies either destroyed or prevented from reaching their final destination.[49]

7. THE FINAL ACT

Although the fighting in Laos was as intense as ever in the second half of 1972, there were growing indications that dramatic changes were in the offing. Not only had Hanoi's gamble for military victory on the battlefield in South Vietnam with the Easter Offensive failed completely, it had provoked the Nixon administration into massive aerial retaliation on a scale unseen before in Southeast Asia. While this was encouraging for the Souvanna government and Vang Pao, because it demonstrated American resolve in the face of North Vietnamese aggression, it also underscored Washington's political desire to be done with the Vietnam War and U.S. military engagement. Now more than ever Laos was simply a bargaining chip—and a very minor one at that—in Washington's exit strategy. Over the next few years, it would be events playing out elsewhere in the Vietnamese peninsula and across the globe, rather than on the battlefield in Laos, that ultimately would seal the fate of the country by 1975.

One Last Chance for Victory

Having once again survived by the skin of his teeth and shored up his defensive positions north of Long Chieng, the irrepressible Vang Pao was ready to go over to the offensive in August and recapture the Plain of Jars. But first he needed an army. His once-proud and fierce fighting force of Hmong soldiers was in tatters following more than three years of unrelenting warfare. Recruits had been harder and harder to find with the decline accelerating as "thousands of Hmong disappeared into their villages and left the war for others to fight."[1] There were some Royal Lao Army troops available, but they were too unreliable. Thus, the burden fell on the roughly 8,000 Thai volunteers attached to his command.

The operation got underway on August 15 with the Seventh Air Force surprisingly being able to provide some 20 F-4s and six A-1s, along with four AC-119s for close air support even as Operation Linebacker (the U.S. air counter-offensive against North Vietnam) was in full swing. Vang Pao's plan called for three independent Thai task forces to seize key terrain south, west, and north of the plain and cut off communist forces from their lines of supply and communication. One task force to the far north, Delta, ran into trouble almost immediately after being airlifted into the Phou San area and was severely mauled by the North Vietnamese. The survivors were forced to fall back across the Nam Ngum River and only saved from complete annihilation by the timely arrival of two emergency Arc Light strikes. Meanwhile, the other two task forces to the south and west were encountering rising resistance and their uncoordinated movements and inability to provide mutual support allowed the enemy to shift forces to defeat each in turn. By mid-September the operation had bogged down.

Never one to give up, Vang Pao launched a diversionary attack in early October by airlifting some 2,000 troops onto the far eastern edge of the plain for an advance up the Ban Ban valley. His goal was to draw enemy troops and reinforcement away from his

The Battle For Laos: Vietnam's Proxy War 1955–1975

A cheerful Vang Pao greets his people in happier times, before the years of fighting took an ever-increasing toll on the Hmong people.

other task forces so they could resume their advance. The North Vietnamese failed to take the bait and instead easily blocked easily this advance with the troops on hand. Eager to salvage something out of his rainy-season offensive, the general sent the newly arrived RLA Mobile Group 32 from Savannakhet on a mission to clear out the enemy along the ridgeline north of Padong. Unfortunately, the 1,500-man unit encountered strong resistance from North Vietnamese and Pathet Lao troops dug in in caves and with supporting artillery and armor. A North Vietnamese counterattack on October 25 inflicted heavy casualties on the attackers: 140 killed and another 143 wounded and missing. Regrouping Mobile Group 32 tried again a week later to take the positon, but was repulsed with the loss of a further 80 dead.[2] Vang Pao finally called it quits in mid-November and began pulling back his troops to the Long Chieng defensive arc.

With the ground fighting over and large numbers of American air assets now available because of the end of Linebacker in October, Seventh Air Force launched a major Barrel Roll interdiction campaign in November. For the first time the state-of-the-art F-111s would be used in Laos. With its advanced avionics and terrain-following technology, the plane was designed to fly at night a mere 200 feet above the ground and could deliver up to 25 conventional 500-pound bombs or 16 cluster bombs accurately on target.[3] Its ability to strike suddenly and without warning earned it the nickname "whispering death" by the North Vietnamese. The plane's capability was further enhanced by introduction of the Sentinel Lock program and its highly accurate radar beacon system. From mid-November until late February 1973, the F-111s flew 2,392 missions with a 91-percent success

The Final Act

In the waning years of the war B-52 Arc Light strikes against communist forces were often the only thing standing between Vang Pao and loss of the Hmong heartland. (Photo U.S. Air Force)

rate and extremely high delivery accuracy using Sentinel Lock, "which was by far the best all-weather delivery system used during the war."[4] The F-111s and B-52s were soon joined by F-4s and A-7 Corsair IIs freed up from Linebacker in pounding the enemy lines of communication and supply depots across the Plain of Jars, while AC-130 gunships conducted nightly truck-hunting missions.

Nonetheless, the North Vietnamese undertook another crack at capturing Long Chieng by launching a dry-season offensive on December 12, 1972. Bypassing most of Vang Pao's outer defenses by sweeping to the west of the Ban Na-Padong line, several thousand North Vietnamese infantry supported by tanks and artillery advanced on Skyline Ridge. Unfortunately for the North Vietnamese, they presented a plum target for American air power. Soon the skies above swarmed with F-4s, A-7s, and AC-130s laying waste to the enemy troop concentrations and artillery sites. In bad weather, B-52s and F-111s took over using Sentinel Lock beacons to relentlessly pound the attackers. Lao T-28s also joined in, flying an additional 2,200 sorties in close air support.[5] Having had enough, the enemy retreated from the battlefield by the end of December.

To the north of the plain another effort was likewise made to capture Bouam Long on Christmas night by three NVA regiments. Once again the defenders held, greatly assisted by American air power. To discourage the enemy from launching further offensive operations, Air Force sorties rose to more than 2,000 in January 1973—half of them by F-4s

The Battle For Laos: Vietnam's Proxy War 1955–1975

The end of military operations over North Vietnam in January 1973 freed up some of America's most advanced aircraft, like the F-111, for duty in Laos. (Photo U.S. Air Force)

and A-7s freed up from an end to operations over North Vietnam.[6] Seeing the writing on the wall and likely low on supplies given the devastation of their supply lines and depots, Hanoi called an early end to its 1972/3 dry-season offensive by February.

Ceasefire

Even as North Vietnamese soldiers in northern Laos were making one last-ditch effort to overrun the Hmong garrison at Bouam Long on Christmas of 1972, their comrades back in the North were desperately gasping for air from the most intense bombing campaign of the war, Linebacker II. Over the course of the previous seven days wave after wave of American B-52 bombers had laid waste to large parts of Hanoi and Haiphong in nightly raids that were then followed by non-stop tactical air strikes during the day. Try as the might, the North's SA-2 missiles and MiG-21 fighters were no match for the Americans. Following eleven days of this air assault in which the heavy bombers unleashed 15,237 tons of bombs on 34 targets across the North Vietnamese heartland,[7] Hanoi agreed to return to the negotiating table in Paris.

The once sluggish negotiations between Henry Kissinger and Le Duc Tho now moved at a swift pace, producing a draft agreement on January 23 with the formal signing of the Paris Peace Accords taking place on January 27, 1973. America's active involvement in the Vietnam War was finally over. But there was no formal mention of Laos; the Laotians would have to work that out among themselves.

The Final Act

The war is over for the United States as the last American troops depart South Vietnam in March 1973.

Thus, the early months of 1973 saw an effort by both the Souvanna government and the Pathet Lao to grab and control as much territory as possible before any ceasefire took hold. While the lines had more or less stabilized in the north, southern Laos saw a push by the North Vietnamese to shore up their position in the panhandle, seizing territory in the Saravane area and on the Bolovens Plateau, to ensure the flow of men and supplies along the Ho Chi Minh Trail into South Vietnam. At Souvanna's request, B-52s made several reprisal strikes, but this did little to change the situation on the ground; the bombers could not stave off collapse, there would be no military salvation.

Ongoing negotiations between Souvanna and Souphanouvong finally produced a ceasefire agreement—the "Agreement on the Restoration of Peace and Reconciliation in Laos"—on February 21, 1973 that was to bring the fighting in Laos to an end. It also provided for the "neutralization" of Luang Prabang and Vientiane (allowing Pathet Lao forces to co-protect these two cities), as well as set the stage for power sharing within a yet-to-be established provincial government.[8] Souvanna was resigned to this fate, but others in his cabinet saw it as a "disguised surrender" and blamed the Americans for coercing the Lao into surrender.[9] They were partially right. A ceasefire had become an end in itself for Washington, another step toward the United States extracting itself from the secret war once and for all. The anti-communist forces would finally be left on their own.

At the time of the ceasefire, the government order of battle stood just shy of 90,000 men, with the Royal Lao Army comprising a little more than half. Vang Pao's roughly 12,000 Hmong fighters and other tribal irregulars accounted for about another quarter and the remaining 16,000 or so were Thai volunteers.[10] Supporting the Lao military was

The Battle For Laos: Vietnam's Proxy War 1955–1975

Pathet Lao forces enter Vientiane with the establishment of a provisional government in September 1973.

a staff of approximately 1,700 Americans, including CIA officers, Air America personnel, and hundreds of uniformed military personnel in Thailand.

The communist forces were slightly larger at just over 108,000 men, but some two-thirds were North Vietnamese troops, the bulk of the 50,000 combat troops coming from three divisions and three independent regiments. Another 21,000 North Vietnamese were attached to the 37,000 Pathet Lao troops as "advisers."[11] Together these communist forces controlled about two-thirds of the country, including nearly all the panhandle, and about one-third of the population at the time of the ceasefire. With the end of fighting the Embassy believed that Hanoi would withdraw its combat troops, but most of the advisers would likely stay on to help sustain the Pathet Lao's military structure, which was as fragile as the government's.[12]

For the large part the ceasefire held. This was more out of war weariness and fatigue than for lack of opportunities, although the communist did make one last land grab in the north by seizing Muong Soui, Sala Phou Khoun, and Tha Viang in mid-April. In response Souvanna requested and received 40 B-52 and 24 F-111 sorties from April 15 to 17, 1973.[13] These would be the last Air Force bombing missions over Laos. From now on RLAF T-28s

The Final Act

U.S. briefing board showing increased communist resupply activity in the Laotian panhandle during 1973 in the aftermath of the American withdrawal from South Vietnam. (Photo Museum of the U.S. Air Force)

would be expected to assume the role of truce-enforcers by bombing or threatening to bomb the Pathet Lao violators. Small-scale clashes and the occasional firefight continued throughout the remaining months of the year as both sides glared at each other across the battle lines while the politicians worked toward negotiating a permanent settlement to the war.

Goodbye Uncle Sam

With the end of U.S. military involvement in Laos in sight, the task at hand was to leave in place a 46,000-man Lao military capable of ensuring the peace. Tribal units would be disbanded, marginal army units dissolved, and an intense retraining program put in place. Special emphasis would be placed on creating a smaller, but quality air force with significant airlift and strike capability. There were more than enough existing aircraft available; in fact the challenge was to downsize while maintaining capability and sustainability. The biggest cut came in the reduction of T-28s from 75 to 25. All this needed to be accomplished on a projected annual U.S. aid budget of between $60 million and $80 million, at a time when Congress was slashing military expenditures for all of Southeast Asia.

The Americans, however, were running out of time. On September 14, 1973 the Souvanna government and the Neo Lao Hak Sat (NLHS), the political wing of the Pathet Lao, signed a political and military protocol prescribing, among other things, a three-step withdrawal of all foreign combat forces, to be completed within 60 days of the formation of a provincial government.[14] Congressional cuts to funding complicated the U.S. effort to leave in place a pro-Western military and provide for the future of Vang Pao's troops, because only a fraction of his men could be integrated into the new army. Despite the Embassy warning in February 1974 that without restored funding Souvanna risked losing the support of Vang Pao, only a modest restoration was achieved.

Moreover, Vang Pao's leadership role was in jeopardy. The Hmong and many of his key commanders had become increasingly disenchanted, feeling abandoned, and rebellious as the once plentiful American funds dried up. The general pleaded his case to Washington for continued funding of the Hmong with the CIA grudgingly acknowledging that "were it not for their association with [the CIA and the U.S. government] their condition today would be vastly less acute than it is."[15]

But the end was near and Vang Pao knew it. The announcement on April 4, 1974 of the formation of the Provisional Government of National Union, which included equal representation for communist and non-communists alike, was the final nail in the coffin. It gave enormous political and military leverage to the NLHS in the new government and all key decisions had to be unanimous, thus guaranteeing government paralysis. Souvanna had been outmaneuvered. "He was naïve and his ego got in the way. He truly believed that his princely status ... and his ability to work out something with his half-brother Souphanouvong [the new vice premier]" meant Laos would not become communist, observed CIA officer Bill Lair.[16]

And the dominos began to fall for the United States. Slowly at first with the last Air America plane flying out of the country on June 3, 1974. A day later the last U.S. military personnel left Laos. The fiscal year 1975 budget provided only $40 million to support the armed forces and even less money flowed to the Hmong. Still, Vang Pao and other pro-Western elements continued to hang on and rebuff ongoing Pathet Lao attempts to nibble away at their territory as best they could. The new year, 1975, ushered in more communist-provoked civil unrest and verbal attacks on an increasingly fragile Souvanna (he suffered a heart attack in early November) and his faction for incompetence and ongoing corruption. The embolden Pathet Lao, now known as the Lao People's Revolutionary Army (LPRA), attacked Royal Lao Army positions near Sala Phou Khoun in early February and Vang Pao responded by bombing them with T-28s. A divided provisional government did nothing to address the growing military tensions and it also proved incapable, or unwilling, to deal with the growing civil unrest as teachers and students joined the protests.

The Final Act

Ceasefire violations continued to mount in the face of increasing LPRA probes, but Vang Pao and other commanders were told to stand down and retreat. This was not in Vang Pao's DNA. He considered himself a Lao patriot, one who had worked hard to integrate the Hmong into Lao society and to support the king and the Royal Lao government throughout his time as a soldier. To this end, he had led his men in destroying $1 billion worth of enemy equipment and in killing thousands of North Vietnamese invaders to protect the Hmong homeland and his country. It had come at a huge cost to the Hmong people: some 17,000 soldiers killed and thousands more wounded, as many as 50,000 civilians killed or wounded, and the loss of their traditional lands and a way of life.[17] And now it was about to all be given away without a fight. So he resisted as best he could, but it was no use.

The Cambodian government of Lon Nol fell to Pol Pot's communist Khmer Rouge on April 17, 1975 and two weeks later North Vietnamese troops entered Saigon as the last American helicopter lifted off the roof of the U.S. Embassy there. On May 9, Souvanna announced that Laos would have to accept "the new realties" in Southeast Asia and he stepped down as premier.[18] Prince Souphanouvong took over and the non-communist members of the provisional government began to flee en masse.

Vang Pao continued to hold on to Long Chieng as he desperately tried to evacuate his people from the coming communist vengeance. An ad hoc airlift was organized by the American and Hmong pilots, but only Vang Pao and some 1,000 of his men and their families would be able to board the few transports that came. The others were left to fend for themselves and make their way to safety across the Mekong into Thailand and exile or flee to the mountains to continue the struggle. It would be every man for himself, as an American official bluntly told Vang Pao that "the United States was washing its hands of the Hmong." It was estimated that some 75,000 Hmong became refugees in Thailand, where they were joined by tens of thousands more Lao fleeing the communist takeover.[19] For them the war was finally over.

The U.S. Embassy continued to function with a small handful of staff and the United States maintained a visible presence even after the communist takeover, but in July 1976 the Souphanouvong government ordered all western military personnel out of the country and thus, more than two decades of American military engagement in Laos came to an end with a whimper.

NOTES

1. The Land of A Million Elephants
1. F. Logevall, *Embers of War*, p. 607.
2. Ibid., p. 242.
3. Ibid., p. 258.
4. Joint Chiefs of Staff, "The Joint Chiefs of Staff and the First Indochina War," p. 121.
5. Ibid., p. 135.
6. V. Anthony and R. Sexton, *The War in Northern Laos*, p. 15.
7. Ibid., p. 19.
8. J. Kurlantzick, *A Great Place to Have a War*, p. 65.
9. Joint Chiefs of Staff, "The Joint Chiefs of Staff and the First Indochina War," p. 15.
10. J. Hamilton-Merritt, *Tragic Mountains*, p. 70.
11. B. Webb, *The Secret War in Laos*, p. 35.
12. T. Castle, *At War in the Shadow of Vietnam*, p. 18.
13. W. Leary, "CIA Air Operations in Laos, 1955–1974."

2. A Nation Divided
1. V. Anthony and R. Sexton, "The War in North Laos, p. 23.
2. L. Nguyen, *Hanoi's War*, p. 45.
3. Ibid.
4. J. Kurlantzick, *A Great Place to Have a War*, p. 70.
5. T. Castle, *At War in the Shadow of Vietnam*, p. 21.
6. Ibid., p. 23; Anthony and Sexton, p. 33.
7. M. Stuart-Fox and M. Kooyman, *Historical Dictionary of Laos*, p. 11.
8. J. Hamilton-Merritt, *Tragic Mountains*, p. 93.
9. Castle, p. 24.
10. "NIE 50-61: Outlook in Mainland Southeast Asia," March 28, 1961.
11. Walt Rostow, as quoted in Castle, p. 27.
12. M. Pribbenow, *Victory in Vietnam*, p. 88.
13. Ibid., pp. 88-9.
14. Castle, p. 42.
15. Kurlantzick, p. 86.
16. N. Hannah, *The Key to Failure*, p. 14.
17. Stuart-Fox and Kooyman, pp. 52-3.
18. Castle, p. 45.
19. Stuart-Fox and Kooyman, p. 10.
20. Castle, p. 56.
21. Anthony and Sexton, p. 104.
22. Ibid., p. 105.
23. Ibid., p. 106.
24. M. McCrea, *U.S. Navy, Marine Corps, and Air Force Fixed-Wing Aircraft Losses and Damage in Southeast Asia (1962–1973)*, Fig. 2-13: Fixed-Wing Aircraft Combat Losses for Combined Services: Total U.S. Aircraft Lost in Laos, p. 2–16.
25. Castle, p.74.

3. Into the Vietnamese Quagmire

1. L. Nguyen, *Hanoi's War*, p. 74.
2. Ibid.
3. S. Emerson, *Air War Over North Vietnam*, pp. 22-3.
4. J. Morrocco, *Thunder From Above*, p. 34.
5. Emerson, p. 78.
6. J. Kurlantzick, *A Great Place to Have a War*, p. 81.
7. Ibid.
8. Castle, p. 34.
9. N. Hannah, *The Key to Failure*, p. 33
10. Castle, p. 77.
11. Ibid., p.78.
12. Ibid.
13. William Sullivan as cited in Castle, p. 77.

4. Raising the Stakes

1. V. Anthony and R. Sexton, *The War in Northern Laos*, p. 153.
2. Ibid.
3. Ibid., p. 155.
4. Ibid., p. 168.
5. Ibid., p. 169.
6. Ibid., p. 170.
7. Ibid., p. 189.
8. T. Castle, *At War in the Shadow of Vietnam*, p. 80; Anthony and Sexton, p. 189.
9. Castle, p. 81.
10. Anthony and Sexton, p. 191.
11. Ibid., p. 192.
12. Ibid., pp. 194-5.
13. Ibid., p. 196.
14. Ibid., p. 209.
15. Ibid., p. 211.
16. Ibid., p. 212.
17. Ibid., pp. 212-14.
18. Ibid., p. 216.
19. Ibid., p. 222.
20. Ibid., p. 222.
21. B. Webb, *The Secret War in Laos*, pp. 216-17.
22. Anthony and Sexton, pp. 228-9.
23. Ibid., p. 231.
24. Ibid., pp. 231 and 234.
25. K. Conboy, *The War in Laos*, p. 7.
26. M. Pribbenow, *Victory in Vietnam*, p. 170.
27. Ibid., pp. 170-1.
28. Ibid., p. 168.
29. J. Van Staaveren, "Interdiction in Southern Laos, p. 56.
30. J. Van Staaveren, "Interdiction in the Laotian Panhandle," p. 104.
31. Ibid., pp. 101-2; Van Staaveren, "Interdiction in the Laotian Panhandle," p. 104.
32. J. Van Staaveren, "Interdiction in Southern Laos, p. 77.
33. C. Hobson, *Vietnam Air Losses*, p. 19.
34. Van Staaveren, "Interdiction in the Laotian Panhandle," p. 105.

35. Ibid.
36. Pribbenow, p. 208.
37. Ibid., p. 182.
38. C. Hobson, *Vietnam Air Losses*, pp. 17-84.
39. Van Staaveren, "Interdiction in the Laotian Panhandle," pp. 108-9.
40. J. Van Staaveren, "Interdiction in Southern Laos," p. 199.
41. Ibid., p. 214.
42. Ibid., p. 215.
43. Ibid., p. 248.
44. Ibid., p. 250.

5. Escalation

1. V. Anthony and R. Sexton, *The War in Northern Laos*, pp. 237-8.
2. Ibid., p. 239.
3. J. Hamilton-Merritt, *Tragic Mountains*, p. 188.
4. Anthony and Sexton, p. 263.
5. Ibid., p. 283.
6. Ibid., p. 285.
7. T. Ahern, *Undercover Armies*, p. 312.
8. Anthony and Sexton, p. 297.
9. Ibid., p. 298.
10. Ibid., p. 298.
11. Ibid., p. 300; C. Hobson, *Vietnam Air Losses*, pp. 177-9.
12. Ahern, p. 315.
13. Anthony and Sexton, pp. 301-2.
14. Ahern, p. 318.
15. Hamilton-Merritt, pp. 213-14.
16. Anthony and Sexton, p. 307.
17. Ibid., p. 309.
18. J. Kurlantzick, *A Great Place to Have a War*, p. 164.
19. Anthony and R. Sexton, pp. 310-11.
20. Ibid., p. 311.
21. Kurlantzick, p. 167.
22. Anthony and Sexton, p. 314.
23. Ibid.
24. Ibid., p. 315; Kurlantzick, p. 168.
25. Anthony and Sexton, p. 315.
26. Kurlantzick, pp. 166-7.
27. Ahern, p. 331.
28. Anthony and Sexton, p. 322.
29. Ibid.
30. W. Westmoreland, *A Soldier Reports*, pp. 409-10.
31. J. Morrocco, *Thunder From Above*, p. 179.
32. J. Olsen, *In Country*, p. 264-5.
33. Morrocco, p. 181; Westmoreland, p. 422.
34. E. Tilford, *Setup*, p. 173.
35. J. Correll, "The Ho Chi Minh Trail," p. 68; J. Sherwood, *Nixon's Trident*, pp. 12-13.
36. Sherwood, p. 13.
37. Hobson, pp. 168-90.
38. B. Nalty, "The War against Trucks," p. 108.

6. The Beginning of the End

1. V. Anthony and R. Sexton, *The War in Northern Laos*, p. 323.
2. M. Pribbenow, *Victory in Vietnam*, p. 254.
3. Anthony and Sexton, p. 324.
4. Ibid., p. 325.
5. Ibid., p. 326.
6. R. Warner, *Back Fire*, p. 287.
7. T. Ahern, *Undercover Armies*, p. 335.
8. Warner, pp. 289-90.
9. Ahern, p. 336.
10. Ibid., p. 330.
11. Ibid., p. 336.
12. Ibid., p. 337.
13. Ahern, p. 343.
14. J. Kurlantzick, *A Great Place to Have a War*, p 191.
15. S. Emerson, *Vietnam's Final Air Campaign*, p. 10.
16. D. Schmitz, *Richard Nixon and the Vietnam War*, p. 84.
17. N. Hannah, *The Key to Failure*, p. 282.
18. Ahern, p. 343.
19. Anthony and Sexton, p. 333.
20. Ibid.
21. Warner, p. 243.
22. Anthony and Sexton, p. 341.
23. Ibid., p. 342.
24. C. Hobson, *Vietnam Air Losses*, pp. 211-17.
25. Anthony and Sexton, p. 345.
26. J. Hamilton-Merritt, *Tragic Mountains*, p. 265.
27. Anthony and Sexton, p. 346.
28. T. Castle, *At War in the Shadow of Vietnam*, p. 107; Pribbenow, p. 287.
29. Anthony and Sexton, p. 351.
30. Ibid., p. 353.
31. Hobson, p. 217.
32. Anthony and Sexton, p. 354.
33. Ahern, p. 438.
34. Ibid., pp. 444-5.
35. Anthony and Sexton, p. 355.
36. Ibid., p. 356.
37. Ahern, p. 454.
38. J. Van Staaveren, "Interdiction in the Laotian Panhandle," p. 111.
39. Ibid.
40. Ibid., p. 114.
41. Pribbenow, p. 274.
42. Van Staaveren, pp. 115-16.
43. B. Nalty, "The War against Trucks," p. 213.
44. Ibid., p. 215.
45. Ibid., p. 218.
46. Ibid.
47. Ibid., p. 219.
48. Van Staaveren, p. 118.
49. Nalty, pp. 232 and 234.

7. The Final Act

1. T. Ahern, *Undercover Armies*, p. 458.
2. Ibid., p. 469.
3. S. Emerson, *Vietnam's Final Air Campaign*, p. 80.
4. V. Anthony and R. Sexton, *The War in Northern Laos*, p. 359.
5. Ibid., pp. 359-60.
6. Ibid., p. 360.
7. Emerson, p. 114.
8. J. Hamilton-Merritt, *Tragic Mountains*, p. 304.
9. Ahern, p. 490.
10. Anthony and Sexton, p. 363.
11. Ibid.
12. Ibid.
13. Ibid., p. 362.
14. Ahern, p. 501.
15. Ibid., p. 497.
16. Hamilton-Merritt, p. 330.
17. Ibid., p. 334.
18. Anthony and Sexton, p. 367.
19. M. Stuart-Fox and M. Kooyman, *Historical Dictionary of Laos*, p. 120.

BIBLIOGRAPHY

Aherns, Thomas. *Undercover Armies: The CIA and Surrogate Warfare in Laos, 1961–1973*. Washington, DC: CIA Center for the Study of Intelligence, 2006.

Anthony, Victor and Richard Sexton. *The United States Air Force in Southeast Asia: The War in Northern Laos, 1954–1973*. Washington, DC: Center for Air Force History, 1993. (Declassified)

Christian Science Monitor, "The Life of General Vang Pao, Hmong Guerrilla Leader," January 11, 2007.

Conboy, Kenneth and Simon McCouaig. *The War in Laos 1960–75*. London: Osprey Publishing, 1989.

Correll, John. "The Ho Chi Minh Trail." *Air Force Magazine*. November 2005.

_____. "The Fall of Lima Site 85." *Air Force Magazine*. April 2006.

Emerson, Stephen. *Air War Over North Vietnam: Operation Rolling Thunder, 1965–1968*. Barnsley, UK: Pen & Sword Military, 2018.

_____. *Vietnam's Final Air Campaign: Operation Linebacker I & II, May–December 1972*. Barnsley, UK: Pen & Sword Military, 2019.

Castle, Timothy. *At War in the Shadow of Vietnam: U.S. Military Aid to the Royal Lao Government, 1955–1975*. New York: Columbia University Press, 1993.

Correll, John. "The Fall of Lima Site 85," *Air Force Magazine*, April 2006.

Hamilton-Merritt, Jane. *Tragic Mountains: The Hmong, the Americans, and the Secret Wars for Laos, 1942–1992*. Bloomington, IN: Indiana University Press, 1999.

Hannah, Norman. *The Key to Failure: Laos & the Vietnam War*. Lanham, MD: Madison Books, 1987.

Hobson, Chris. *Vietnam Air Losses. United States Air Force, Navy and Marine Corps Fixed-Wing Aircraft Losses in Southeast Asia 1961–1975*. Hinckley, UK: Midland Publishing, 2001.

Kurlantzick, Joshua. *A Great Place to Have a War: America in Laos and the Birth of a Military CIA*. New York: Simon & Schuster, 2016.

Leary, William. "CIA Operations in Laos, 1955–1974: Supporting the Secret War." Washington, DC: CIA Center for the Study of Intelligence, Winter 1999–2000.

Logevall, Fredrik. *Embers of War: The Fall of an Empire and the Making of America's Vietnam*. New York: Random House, 2013.

McCrea, Michael. *U.S. Navy, Marine Corps, and Air Force Fixed-Wing Aircraft Losses and Damage in Southeast Asia (1962–1973)*. Arlington, VA: Center for Naval Analysis, August 1976.

Morrocco, John. *The Vietnam Experience: Rain of Fire, Air War 1969–1973*. Boston: Boston Publishing Company, 1985.

Nalty, Bernard. "The War against Trucks: Aerial Interdiction in Southern Laos, 1968-1972." Washington, DC: Air Force History and Museums Program, 2005.

New York Times Magazine, "Gen. Vang Pao's Last War;" May 11, 2008.

Nguyen, Lien-Hang. *Hanoi's War: An International History of the War for Peace in Vietnam.* Chapel Hill, NC: University of North Carolina Press, 2012.

Office of the Chairman of the Joint Chiefs of Staff. *The Joint Chiefs of Staff and the First Indochina War, 1947–1954.* Washington, DC: Office of Joint History, 2004.

Olsen, James. *In Country: The Illustrated Encyclopedia of the Vietnam War.* New York: Metro Books, 2008.

Pribbenow, Merle (translator). *Victory in Vietnam. The Official History of the People's Army of Vietnam, 1954–1975.* Lawrence, KS: University Press of Kansas, 2002.

Schmitz, David. *Richard Nixon and the Vietnam War.* Lanham, MD: Rowman & Littlefield, 2016.

Sherwood, John. *Nixon's Trident: Naval Power in Southeast Asia, 1968–1972.* Washington, DC: Naval History & Heritage Command, 2009.

Stuart-Fox, Martin and Mary Kooyman. *Historical Dictionary of Laos.* Metuchen, NJ: The Scarecrow Press, 1992.

U.S. Department of State. "NIE 50-61: Outlook in Mainland Southeast Asia," March 28, 1961. *Foreign Relations of the United States, 1961–1963,* Volume XXIII, *Southeast Asia.* Found at https://history.state.gov/historicaldocuments/frus1961-63v23/d2

Vang, Chia Youyee. *Fly Until You Die: An Oral History of Hmong Pilots in the Vietnam War.* New York: Oxford University Press, 2019.

Van Staaveren, Jacob. "Interdiction in the Laotian Panhandle" in Carl Berger (ed.) *The United States Air Force in Southeast Asia, 1961–1973.* Washington, DC: Office of Air Force History, 1984.

_____. "Interdiction in Southern Laos, 1960-1968." Washington, DC: Center for Air Force History, 1993.

Warner, Roger. *Back Fire: The CIA's Secret War in Laos and Its Link to the War in Vietnam.* New York: Simon & Schuster, 1995.

Webb, Billy. *The Secret War in Laos and General Vang Pao, 1958–1975.* Xlibris, 2016.

Westmoreland, William. *A Soldier Reports.* Garden City, NJ: Doubleday & Co., 1976.

Index

Air America 16, 26, 34, 35, 41, 49, 51-54, 57, 70, 72, 79, 98, 100, 114
   creation of 16, 26, 34
   pilots 15, 26, 33, 34, 54, 89, 114
   Udorn complex 15, 34, 42, 51, 53, 55, 57, 71, 92, 95, 96
air defenses (Laos) 33, 61, 63, 66, 83, 85, 88, 89, 96, 97, 100, 101, 106-108
   antiaircraft weaponry 33, 61, 63, 66, 83, 85, 88, 89, 96, 100, 101, 106-108
   in panhandle 97, 85, 86, 88, 106, 107
   SA-2 surface-to-air missiles 106, 108, 112
aircraft losses 33, 66, 71, 85, 89, 105, 108
Air Force, U.S. 26, 30, 33, 38, 41, 46, 49, 60, 65, 71, 96
   Seventh Air Force 54, 55, 61, 62, 73, 81, 54, 85, 89, 91-93, 95, 97, 98, 100, 102, 105, 109, 110
   bases in Thailand 33, 46, 49, 52, 54, 55, 69, 71, 101
Arc Light 66, 67, 69, 86, 109, 111
armed reconnaissance 65, 68, 82, 88

Ban Ban 23, 49, 78, 82, 84, 85, 109
bombing 33, 35, 51, 61, 65-71, 77, 83, 84, 86, 87, 90-92, 96, 102, 106, 112, 114-116
   blocking belts 88, 90, 106
   chokepoints 65, 68, 82, 83, 85, 88, 89, 102
   close air support 53, 54, 56-58, 78, 85, 86, 92, 96, 97, 102, 103, 109, 111
   decision-making, U.S. 41, 45, 46, 106, 116
   interdiction 41, 56, 61, 62, 63, 65-69, 82, 83, 85, 87-89, 91, 93, 95, 97, 98, 100, 102, 03, 105, 108, 110
   napalm use 52, 59, 73, 74
Bouam Long 75, 77, 83, 93, 98, 111, 112

Cambodia 17, 95, 103, 106, 107
   Lon Nol 95, 117
China 18, 23, 25, 28, 34
CIA 26, 28, 32, 34, 38-43, 46, 48, 50, 53, 55, 62, 66, 71-73, 76, 79, 84, 89, 92-93, 95, 100, 101, 103, 114, 116
   field officers 41, 50, 53, 72, 73, 75, 76, 79, 94, 114, 116

Operation Momentum 38, 40, 43
   and Ambassador William Sullivan 41, 45, 46, 49, 54, 59, 61, 65, 68, 69, 72, 119
   road-watch teams 55, 62, 66
   and Vang Pao 28, 39, 43, 53
coalition governments 12-14, 19, 23, 29, 30, 32
Congress, U.S. 94, 95, 116
   war funding and restrictions 94, 95, 116
corruption 14, 15, 22, 116

Department of State, U.S. 42, 69, 80, 89
Dien Bien Phu 8, 10, 11, 12, 59, 62, 101

Easter Offensive (1972) 102, 108, 109

forward air controllers see also Ravens 35, 52, 57, 61, 62, 66, 68, 73, 83, 84, 86, 88, 100, 101

Geneva Accords 12, 13, 15, 16, 25, 27, 30, 40, 42, 45
   1954 12, 13, 15, 16, 25, 27, 30
   1962 40, 42, 45
Group 559 (North Vietnam) 20, 25, 56, 63, 66

Hmong see also Vang Pao 24-28, 34, 38-40, 43, 46, 48-50, 52, 53, 57-59, 61, 70-77, 79-84, 90, 91, 92, 94, 97, 99, 100-102, 109, 111-113, 116, 117
   irregulars 24, 28, 46, 113
   Long Chieng headquarters 26, 76, 77, 81, 92, 94, 96-98, 100-102, 109-111, 117
   military operations 26, 43, 58, 59, 72-77, 79-84, 90, 97, 100
   pilots 80, 96, 102, 117
   refugees 34, 43, 62, 70, 117
Ho Chi Minh 7, 8, 14, 17
Ho Chi Minh Trail see also Group 559; Operation Steel Tiger; Operation Commando Hunt 17, 20, 37, 41, 45, 49, 54-56, 62, 63, 65, 66, 68, 78, 80, 81, 83, 85, 87-89, 101, 106, 107, 108, 111, 113
   construction of 20, 21
   supply flows 41, 54, 62, 63, 65, 78, 89, 113
   Tchepone logistics hub 25, 47, 103, 105
   truck kills 49, 55, 56, 61, 62, 65, 66, 68, 80, 83, 85, 87-89, 101, 106, 107, 108, 111

Johnson, Lyndon 36-38, 45, 46, 51, 87

Kennedy, John 23-25, 27, 29, 31, 42
Khang Khay 23, 28, 31, 33, 54, 56, 80, 84
King Savang Vatthana 18, 20, 22, 90, 98
King Sisavang Vong 7, 11, 12, 20
Kissinger, Henry 112
    and Paris peace talks 112
Kong Le *see also* Neutralist forces 22-24, 31-33, 39, 45, 51, 52, 55
Kouprasith Abhay 23, 32, 48

Lam Son 719 103, 105-107
Le Duan 36-38
Lima sites 26, 34, 48-50, 54, 61, 70, 73, 74, 76, 77, 83, 93, 97, 98
    LS 15 93, 97
    LS 32 77, 93, 98
    LS 36 49, 50, 54, 70, 76
    LS 58 48, 49
    LS 85 26, 73
    LS 107 74
    LS 115 83
Long Chieng 26, 76, 77, 81, 92, 94, 96-98, 100-102, 109-111, 117
Luang Prabang 7, 8, 11, 22, 24, 26, 31, 35, 39, 52, 55, 57, 58, 60-63, 81 113

Military Assistance Command, Vietnam (MACV) 45, 49, 54, 66, 89, 91
military regions 43, 48, 79
Momyer, William 55, 65, 67, 73, 86
Moua Cher Pao 78, 93, 98
mountain passes
    Ban Karai 65, 88, 106
    Ban Raving 65, 106
    Barthelemy 59
    Mu Gia 65, 66, 69, 88, 106-108
    Nape 65
Muong Soui 32, 33, 35, 49, 51, 52, 54, 56, 59, 76-82, 84, 91, 93, 96, 97, 114

Nakhon Phanom air base (Thailand) 53, 55, 60, 68, 73, 82, 87, 95, 97, 101, 106
Na Khang 49, 50, 52, 54, 56, 59, 70, 73-76
Nam Bac 55, 56, 58, 59, 61, 62, 70

Nam Ngum River 109
Nam Tha 29
Navy, U.S. 33, 41, 49-51, 54, 55, 59, 61, 74, 78, 85, 93, 95, 110
    Operation Barrel Roll 41, 49-51, 54, 55, 59, 61, 74, 78, 85, 93, 95, 110
    Yankee Team reconnaissance 33
Neutralist forces *see also* Kong Le 27, 28, 30-33, 35, 41, 51-56, 59, 78-81, 84, 91
neutralization of Laos 113
Nixon, Richard 89, 91, 94, 95, 109
    and Henry Kissinger 112
    Paris peace talks 43, 112
Nong Pet 82, 83
North Vietnam 15-20, 25-28, 29, 32, 35-41, 43, 46, 48, 51, 52, 55, 56, 61, 63, 65, 66, 68, 69, 71, 81, 82, 87, 94, 95, 106, 109-114, 117
    aid to Pathet Lao 7, 13-15, 20, 25, 28, 29, 46, 48, 73
    and Prince Souphanouvong 13, 17, 19, 20, 32, 117
North Vietnamese Army 16, 19, 43, 46, 48, 52, 56, 57, 58, 62, 70, 71, 74, 76, 78, 81, 85, 86, 90-93, 95, 97, 98, 100, 105, 111, 112, 114, 117
    312th Division 78, 91, 98, 100
    316th Division 76, 81, 85, 92, 98
    Campaign 319 91
    Campaign Total Victory 78
    Campaign Z 98

Operation About Face 79-81, 83, 85, 90, 98
Operation Barrel Roll 41, 49-51, 54, 55, 59, 61, 74, 78, 85, 93, 95, 110
Operation Commando Hunt 88, 89, 95, 103, 105, 106, 108
Operation Igloo White 82, 87, 88, 103, 106
Operation Linebacker 109-112
Operation Momentum 38, 40, 43
Operation Prasane 55
Operation Pig Fat 74
Operation Rain Dance 76-78, 81, 82
Operation Rolling Thunder 38, 54, 61, 70, 71, 87
Operation Steel Tiger 41, 54, 55, 62, 65-69, 87, 105

Padong 26, 28, 29, 40, 110, 111
Paris Peace Accord (1973) *see also* peace negotiations 43, 112

Index

Pathet Lao *see also* Prince Souphanouvong 7, 10, 11, 13-20, 22-33, 35, 39-43, 46, 48, 52, 55, 56, 59, 61, 62, 71, 73, 74, 77, 78, 80, 81, 90, 98, 110, 113-116
peace negotiations 11, 35, 43, 112
    and Easter Offensive 108, 109
    and Henry Kissinger 112
Phong Savan 84, 98
Phoumi Nosavan 20, 22-25, 29-32, 48
Plain of Jars 11, 23, 27, 31, 33, 35, 39-41, 43, 48, 50-54, 56, 75-77, 78, 81, 82, 84, 85, 90, 91, 78, 98, 102, 109, 111
Prince Boun Oum 22-24, 28, 29
Prince Souphanouvong 13, 17, 19, 20, 32, 117
Prince Souvanna 13-15, 17-20, 22, 23, 29-33, 40, 41, 46, 52, 59, 62, 65, 68, 76, 80, 81, 90, 91, 97, 98, 109, 113, 114, 116, 117
Project Water Pump 42, 96

Ravens *see also* forward air controllers 52, 57, 100, 101
Royal Armed Forces (FAR) 28, 29, 31, 32, 35, 41, 46, 48, 52-56, 58, 59, 62, 79, 80, 82, 84, 91, 92, 97, 102
Royal Lao Air Force (RLAF) *see also* Thao Ma 7, 33, 35, 41, 49, 51, 53, 55, 58-60, 62, 63, 74, 77-79, 83, 85, 90, 91, 93, 95-97, 101, 114
Royal Lao Army (RLA) 7, 15, 97, 100, 109, 110, 113, 116

Sam Neua 11, 13, 19, 20, 24, 48, 49, 57, 59, 61, 70, 71, 74, 81
Sam Thong 91, 92, 100-102
Saravane 26, 102, 113
Savannakhet Province 22, 26, 68, 110
Skyline Ridge 26, 92, 97, 100, 102, 111
SLAM strikes 67
South Vietnam *see also* Tet and Easter offensives 12, 15, 17, 20, 33, 35-39, 44-49, 63, 65-67, 69, 70, 85, 86, 89, 94, 95, 102, 103, 105-109, 113
    Khe Sanh, battle of 85, 86

Lam Son 719 103, 105-107
    U.S. troop levels 94; troop withdrawals 89, 90, 95, 103, 113, 115
    and Vietnamization 89, 91, 94, 95, 103
Soviet Union 18, 23-25, 31, 45, 100
Sullivan, William 41, 45, 46, 49, 54, 59, 61, 65, 68, 69, 72, 119

Tchepone 25, 47, 103, 105
Tet Offensive (1968) 69, 86, 87, 105
Thailand 15, 29, 33-35, 40, 43, 45, 46, 48, 49, 51-55, 65, 69, 71, 101, 114, 117
    air bases 33, 46, 49, 52, 54, 55, 69, 71, 101
        Korat 50, 52
        Nakhon Phanom 53, 55, 60, 68, 73, 82, 87, 95, 97, 101, 106
        Takhil 66
        Udorn 15, 34, 35, 42, 51, 53, 55, 57, 71, 92, 95, 96
        U-Tapao 69, 91, 100
        Project Water Pump
Thao Ma *see also* Royal Lao Air Force 42, 96

Udorn air base (Thailand) 15, 34, 35, 42, 51, 53, 55, 57, 71, 92, 95, 96

Vang Pao 28, 29, 32, 34, 39, 40, 43, 46, 48-59, 70, 73-85, 90-94, 96-98, 100-102, 109-111, 113, 116, 117
Vientiane 7, 15, 16, 19, 20, 22-24, 32, 33, 39, 48, 49, 52, 53, 55, 69, 76, 81, 101, 113, 114
Viet Cong 37, 38, 86, 87, 95
Vietnamization *see also* United States; South Vietnam 89, 91, 94, 95, 103
Vo Nguyen Giap 11

Westmoreland, William 54, 65, 66, 69, 86

Xieng Khouang Province 24, 31, 56
Xieng Khouangville 23, 24, 77, 78, 81, 84, 91, 98

Acknowledgements

Special thanks to the National Museum of the Air Force in Dayton, Ohio and especially to archivist Brett Stolle for his invaluable assistance in helping me research the museum's data and photo collections.

My deep appreciation to all the writers and researchers before me who have written about the war in Laos and American involvement there, without them this undertaking would have been near impossible. Special recognition is given to Victor Anthony and Richard Sexton's *The War in Northern Laos*, Thomas Aherns' *Undercover Armies*, Roger Warner's *Back Fire*; Jane Hamilton-Merritt's *Tragic Mountains*, and the work of Jacob Van Staaveren on U.S. interdiction operations in the Laotian panhandle. Chia Youyee Vang's story of the Hmong pilots, *Fly Until You Die*, provides a fascinating look at a neglected aspect of the war.

Finally, in the telling of the Laotian civil war one cannot be moved by the high cost paid by the Lao people, who found themselves and their country caught up in a geopolitical struggle not of their own making. They truly became pawns in this Cold War confrontation. The Hmong people in particular, risked it all in the name of the anti-communist struggle at the behest of the United States and paid a dear price—both during and after the war. Their sacrifice should not be forgotten.

Stephen Emerson was born in San Diego, California into a U.S. Navy family; his father was a career naval aviator and his mother a former Navy nurse. Steve and his siblings grew up on various Navy bases during the Vietnam War. His father served two combat tours as an attack pilot in Vietnam flying the A-4 Skyhawk as part of Operation Rolling Thunder while flying off the USS *Midway* in 1965 with VA-22 and later as commanding officer of VA-146 flying the A-7 Corsair II while embarked on the USS *Enterprise* in 1969. Steve holds a Ph.D. in International Relations/Comparative Politics from the University of Florida and currently resides in Orlando, Florida. His recent books, *Air War Over North Vietnam: Operation Rolling Thunder, 1965–1968* and *Air War Over North Vietnam: Operation Rolling Thunder, 1965–1968*, examine American efforts to use air power as a tool of coercive diplomacy.